Limiting Beliefs

How to Overcome Limiting Beliefs and Tap Your Potential

(How to Rewire Your Brain Stop Overthinking Develop Mental Toughness)

Eugene Lazaro

Published By **Jenna Olsen**

Eugene Lazaro

All Rights Reserved

Limiting Beliefs: How to Overcome Limiting Beliefs and Tap Your Potential (How to Rewire Your Brain Stop Overthinking Develop Mental Toughness)

ISBN 978-1-7382986-9-3

Table Of Contents

Chapter 1: Breaking Free 1

Chapter 2: Dampening The Joys Of Life ..17

Chapter 3: Behavioral Activation 31

Chapter 4: Practical Strategies to Leverage Neuro Plasticity 47

Chapter 5: Challenge Negative Thoughts 64

Chapter 6: Mental Toughness in Action..74

Chapter 7: Mastering Your Response......86

Chapter 8: Battling Self-Doubt 97

Chapter 9: Understanding the Power of Beliefs...111

Chapter 10: Overcoming Self-Doubt 118

Chapter 11: Creating A Supportive Environment 131

Chapter 12: Cultivating Self-Compassion 144

Chapter 13: Mindfulness and Creativity 151

Chapter 14: Acknowledging the Mountain Within 159

Chapter 15: Identifying Self-Limiting Beliefs.. 173

Chapter 16: Overcoming Self Doubt 180

Chapter 1: Breaking Free

Have you ever determined yourself paralyzed with the aid of manner of self-doubt? An opportunity or aspiration surfaces, but rather than charging ahead, you sense a shroud of worry and uncertainty descend upon you. Thoughts like, "I'm no longer capable enough," "I'm sure to fail," or "People will determine me," echo in your mind, restraining you from pursuing your dreams. These are examples of proscribing beliefs.

A curious aggregate of creativity and boundless imagination defined my early life. As a long way as I can don't forget, I commonly had an undeniable passion for developing art work. I cherished the tranquil hours spent on my own, brushing colorful shades onto a clean canvas, reworking it right into a tapestry of my coronary heart's expressions. Every stroke modified into a testimony to my creativity and a delivery of deep delight.

One day, underneath the scrutinizing gaze of my art trainer, this narrative modified. "This isn't real sufficient, Luna," she stated, searching at one among my paintings with a nonchalant shrug. Her terms, meant to be a critique, took on a existence in their very own. They weaved themselves into the essence of my being, manifesting as a crippling self-doubt that began to overshadow my love for artwork. I started to question my abilities and my knowledge. And slowly, the canvases remained easy, the brushes dried, and the colors faded.

This unmarried remark from my artwork instructor catalyzed a massive personal paradigm shift. My limiting beliefs took root inside the fertile soil of this critique and commenced branching out to one of kind areas of my life. Every aspiration regarded too a protracted way-fetched, each dream too grand, every threat too precarious. This paralyzing fear of no longer being "perfect sufficient" determined me like an ominous shadow, making me maintain back, and preventing me from pursuing my dreams.

Is this narrative familiar to you? Do you too convey the weight of self-doubt that keeps you from know-how your dreams? We frequently underestimate the strength of limiting beliefs in our lives. They lurk in the recesses of our minds, whispering words of fear and failure, nudging us a ways from the route of risks and possibilities.

Fast in advance to my maturity, my dream of practicing existence education emerged. The delight ends up palpable, as have become the echoing chorus of self-doubt. The antique chorus achieved in my thoughts, "You're no longer appropriate enough. You'll fail. People won't take shipping of as actual with an inexperienced teach which include you."

My restricting ideals, born from a casual statement in an art work splendor, have been now towering round me. The course to my desires gave the look of a bewildering maze, each flip essential to a dull stop. But with time and lots introspection, I placed out these partitions had been no longer made from stone or concrete; they had been self-imposed obstacles of my very own making, and it become in my electricity to dismantle them, brick with the useful aid of brick.

You can also have experienced comparable struggles, allow opportunities bypass via, and allow dreams live actually goals, all because your self-doubt whispered, "You cannot." The pain and remorse that encompass statistics you have were given held once more from achieving for what you certainly desire must moreover be acquainted.

Over time, through ordinary strive and the right mind-set, I controlled to dismantle those barriers. Please accept as true with that you could too; it's miles why I wrote this e-book. This journey is set spotting your proscribing beliefs, tough them, and ultimately breaking unfastened. I'll manual you thru it using sensible, effective techniques that have converted my lifestyles and those of my clients.

Identifying and overcoming proscribing ideals is like doing away with the handcuffs that have been restraining your functionality. Imagine sooner or later being loose to run within the direction of your desires with a renewed self notion and resilience that nothing can deter. That is the purpose of this e-book: to launch you from the shackles of self-doubt and limiting beliefs and permit your unrealized capability to dance.

Before we're in a position to overcome those limiting thoughts, we have to outline them. What hold us lower lower back are our preconceived notions of who we are and the location round us. They are commonly ingrained within the direction of our early years, and through the years, come to be so routine that we slightly be aware their presence, no longer to say task them. For instance, in case you grew up in an environment wherein making mistakes become critically punished, you may grow up with the limiting notion that "If I make a mistake, I am a failure." This belief can maintain you once more from trying new reports or taking over disturbing conditions because of the fear of failure.

Understanding the origins of those restricting beliefs can assist in overcoming them. They frequently stem from our childhood reminiscences, family values, and schooling and also are extensively stimulated with the resource of social conditioning—the norms, values, and ideals that society imposes on us. For example, societal requirements of beauty or fulfillment can domesticate proscribing ideals which include, "I'm no longer lovely enough" or "I'm not a fulfillment until I really have a positive hobby or amount of wealth."

The route to freedom starts offevolved offevolved with attention. By developing a conscious attempt to find out and understand your limiting ideals, you start the method of deconstructing them. Remember, every wall is manufactured from man or woman bricks. By doing away with each brick—each proscribing perception—one after the alternative, we can carry down the partitions that confine us.

In the following pages, we are able to circulate into the inner depths of our psyche to discover the results of these proscribing beliefs on our lives, and most importantly, how we are capable of begin to overcome them. Prepare for a adventure that allows you to supply you toward your proper self, one in every of transformation and boom. Hold tight; the road is probably difficult, however the rewards are beyond diploma. As you switch the pages of this e-book, keep in mind that each phrase and each workout is a step toward your freedom and a existence freed from proscribing ideals.

Your journey to breaking free begins offevolved now.

1A. UNDERSTANDING THE ROOT OF LIMITING BELIEFS

Like a farmer plucking weeds from the soil, you need to understand those adverse mind in advance than you could start getting rid of them. Limiting ideals are insidious. They are lousy narratives that exist to your subconscious, directing your actions, decisions, and perceptions of your self and your capabilities. They constantly whisper, "You can't do it" or "It's more stable no longer to attempt," and permeate each place of our lives, inhibiting private increase and ability.

You ought to possibly apprehend some of the ones restricting beliefs as they echo on your mind: "I have to be pleasant to be fashionable," "I normally lessen to rubble," or "Success is meant for others, now not for me." These thoughts, which we regularly take shipping of with out question, bind us and restriction our ability to development.

The Roots of Your Limiting Beliefs

Your limiting ideals have roots. They are not spontaneous apparitions and are often rooted in your younger humans research and early learning. Family values and beliefs extensively impact those thoughts. For example, if your family valued conformity over individuality, you probable grew up believing you had to aggregate in to be commonplace. If success have become overemphasized, you likely internalized the perception that your truly worth is tied on your achievement, making failure an unacceptable, devastating prospect.

Life opinions moreover play a massive function in forming those deep-rooted ideals. A single awful come across, which encompass failing a test, can plant the seed of a limiting perception like "I'm no longer clever sufficient." Over time, if such thoughts are not challenged, they might solidify, affecting yourself warranty on your intellectual abilties and, therefore, your educational or professional interests.

Education is a top notch sized contributor to our limiting beliefs too. You can also have had a instructor who bellevaed that best powerful people are innovative or that math is a subject only some brains are forced for. Without identifying it, you may have adopted these beliefs as reality, installing invisible limitations for yourself.

The Impact of Social Conditioning

It's now not simply your personal reviews and found out values that form those limiting beliefs. Social conditioning performs a pivotal function in their formation. Society, frequently thru media, promotes precise narratives and requirements. It perpetuates first-rate stereotypes like "Men do now not cry" or establishes superficial requirements of splendor, leading to beliefs like "I'm no longer appealing sufficient." These societal expectations and norms exert stress, shaping our perceptions of ourselves and what we deem functionality or appropriate.

Take a second and reflect on those elements. What circle of relatives values had been instilled in you developing up? How would possibly your beyond reviews or education have contributed to any self-doubt or fears you face in recent times? In what way has societal conditioning inspired yourself-notion? The answers to those questions can also bring on a number of your very very own limiting ideals.

It is important to remember that the ones ideals aren't concrete truths but certainly perceptions, shaped with the aid of severa factors over the years. As such, they will be reshaped and modified with empowering ideals that sell boom and freedom. In the subsequent chapters, we are able to find out sensible strategies to deconstruct these limitations and update them with beliefs that serve you and align together at the side of your unlocked capacity.

The Promise of Personal Transformation

This journey may appear daunting at the beginning but take into account that discomfort frequently accompanies increase. Embrace the pain you revel in along the manner because of the reality it is proof of the way a protracted way you have come. I and numerous others have braved this direction in advance than, and I promise you that you can now not simplest go through the pain however furthermore redesign into your top notch self. Challenging your ingrained, included responses and actively changing your attitudes and conduct are vital steps inside the course of reshaping your whole identification and overcoming your restricting beliefs. Through each warfare and triumph, you may discover your self shifting toward a life no longer ruled by fear or self-doubt however thru using self-guarantee, resilience, and success. This is your journey to overcoming your proscribing ideals, and it begins right right right here, proper now.

How Limiting Beliefs Impact Our Lives

Diving deeper, allow's in addition dissect how the ones restricting ideals, commonplace by means of the mentioned factors, can effect our each day lives. These internal boundaries do no longer exist in a vacuum. They intertwine with yourself-perception, actions, and responses to life activities and ultimately, form your truth. For example, in case you harbor the notion that "I'm no longer a human beings man or woman," it could deter you from in search of or playing social interactions, which can purpose feelings of loneliness or isolation.

Limiting ideals may be in particular unfavourable in the context of personal or profession growth. If you're glad that "I'm now not leadership fabric," you are probably to pull away from possibilities for development, thereby stagnating your professional improvement. This self-restricting narrative continues you stuck in your consolation location, preventing you from figuring out your complete functionality.

The Emotional Toll of Limiting Beliefs

Our restricting beliefs moreover effect our feelings. They can extend emotions of stress, anxiety, and dissatisfaction as we continuously warfare to fulfill the unrealistic requirements we've got set for ourselves. For instance, the perception "I have to be incredible to be loved" can cause regular self-complaint and feelings of inadequacy, affecting our relationships and intellectual health.

It's crucial to understand that proscribing ideals are not constantly openly horrible. They also can appear defensive or maybe low-priced. You might likely inform yourself that you avoid making speeches due to the reality "it is just no longer your detail." On the ground, this belief may appear threat loose, a easy elegance of your alternatives. But if it's far born out of fear of judgment or failure, it is a proscribing belief preventing you from developing a functionality or achieving personal increase.

Furthermore, our proscribing ideals may additionally have a domino effect. One limiting notion can make more potent others, developing a dense internet of self-doubt and fear. For instance, if you remember that "I'm no longer incredible enough," it could reason first-rate proscribing ideals along aspect "I do no longer deserve success" or "No one will love me." Over time, those intertwined beliefs can generate a self-enjoyable prophecy. Your moves, driven with the aid of using the ones beliefs, will align with them, reinforcing their perceived validity.

Understanding the amount of the impact of such limiting ideals on our lives is crucial to overcoming them. They no longer exceptional forestall our personal and professional boom but moreover impact our emotional well-being and brilliant of existence.

I want you to take a second and consider a life loose from those constraints. A lifestyles wherein you are not held lower decrease again via the use of worry or self-doubt, one in which you're assured, resilient, and unafraid to pursue your dreams and passions. This lifestyles isn't always a mere myth; you can make it. But to gain it, you need to first confront your restricting ideals, understand their roots, and steadily discover ways to replace them with empowering ideals that promote non-public boom and happiness.

Let's step collectively right into a global wherein you are not confined through using your doubts but empowered with the useful resource of your competencies and functionality. However, in advance than we dive in, it's miles critical to recognize the amount of the toll that those limiting beliefs tackle our lives.

Chapter 2: Dampening The Joys Of Life

Even the simple joys of lifestyles may be tarnished through those beliefs. For instance, the perception that "I have to usually be effective" may want to make you enjoy answerable for taking day out for leisure sports activities, robbing you of the pleasure and relaxation they create.

Furthermore, restricting ideals also can kill off originality and imagination. If you don't forget that "I'm not a revolutionary man or woman" or "my mind are not proper sufficient," you may withhold your mind and mind and chorus from contributing for your complete ability to your private and professional existence. This is not just a loss for you however moreover for parents who've to advantage from your precise insights and thoughts.

Overall, the charges of limiting beliefs taint each aspect of our lives. They stable a dark cloud over our capability for growth, achievement, and happiness. However, spotting the ones charges is step one within the course of liberation. As we adventure through this eBook, I will offer you with the gadget and strategies to promote off these heavy stones from your backpack and make your journey via lifestyles lighter, freer, and more amusing.

1C. PEELING BACK THE LAYERS: STRATEGIES FOR UNCOVERING YOU'RE LIMITING BELIEFS

Unearthing our limiting ideals is similar to peeling decrease lower back the layers of an onion. We start at the floor, but as we do the inner artwork, we encounter more profound, frequently hidden elements of ourselves. It's essential to understand that this method calls for honesty and bravery as you're approximately to embark on a adventure of self-discovery. This journey would possibly in all likelihood every now and then be tough, but it is crucial to consider that self-attention is the first step to overcoming our proscribing beliefs. Once we're aware of the ones subconscious assumptions, we are capable of begin to query and replace them with greater brilliant, increase-selling ideals.

Before we bounce into unique strategies, it's miles vital to domesticate an attitude of non-judgmental interest in the course of your thoughts and beliefs. Permit yourself to think freely and without criticism. Remember, those beliefs have been fashioned without your aware choice, so blaming yourself for having them serves no purpose aside from to create a in addition proscribing perception!

First Technique: The Out-Of-Body Method

As we delve into our exploration of uncovering limiting ideals, one technique this is specifically illuminating is the "Out-of-Body" technique This approach, which might also additionally appear normal earlier than the whole lot, taps into the power of statement, allowing us to become indifferent visitors of our very personal lives.

Much like a director severely reading a scene from a film, the Out-of-Body approach invitations you to adopt a 3rd-character thoughts-set towards yourself As you step out of doors your right now studies and feelings, you begin to observe your actions and reactions as an outsider ought to. It's as despite the fact that you're looking a movie of your existence playing out, looking your individual with hobby, compassion, and statistics. This change of mind-set can provide placing insights that can otherwise be omitted within the thick of personal involvement.

The thriller to this technique is based on observing styles in your conduct. Let's keep in mind an instance. Suppose you word that every time you are offered a manipulate position at paintings, you decline and advocate someone else absorb the possibility, despite the fact that you're in reality licensed for the characteristic. From an outside attitude, you will probably look at this repeated movement and start to impeach why you usually bypass such opportunities. Is it because of a lack of self guarantee or fear of failure? Or perhaps a belief which you're no longer deserving of a management characteristic? These questions can lead you to unearth the proscribing perception that "I'm now not in a function sufficient to influence."

This method moreover calls for a keen interest at the situations that cause you misery or lead you to act in procedures that contradict your real goals. Such moments of pain and resistance are frequently revealing. For example, in case you find out yourself feeling deeply traumatic at some point of social gatherings, no matter the reality which you without a doubt enjoy socializing, you can begin to query what's at the premise of this tension. Could or now not it is a worry of judgment Or perhaps a perception which you're inherently stupid? By making use of the Out-of-Body technique, you could perceive the functionality proscribing perception "People won't discover me exciting."

Furthermore, this technique lets in you to discover the ability triggers for the ones ideals. Using our preceding example, you would possibly have a take a look at that your anxiety during social gatherings spikes on the same time as you're spherical sure folks that seem mainly judgmental or while you're expected to talk about yourself. Recognizing the ones triggers can provide extra clues to the restricting ideals hidden under the floor.

Second Technique: The Fill-In-The-Blank Method

The second method is "The Fill-in-the-Blank" technique. This introspective method flourishes on self-interrogation and honesty because it makes use of an easy however powerful fill-in-the-easy declaration: 'I cannot attain/bee/have _____ because of the reality _____.'

This method is like venturing into the wooded vicinity of your thoughts, prepared with a highbrow flashlight. Each 'easy' inside the statement represents an unexplored corner that might be home to a limiting perception. By illuminating the ones corners, you are likely to unearth beliefs that you were previously blind to or had been sidestepping.

To illustrate how this technique works, permit's taken into account some examples. Imagine you have constantly dreamt of beginning your very own business corporation, but every time the possibility arises, you locate reasons to postpone it. If you have got been to finish the announcement, it'd look something like this: "I can't begin my very own agency because of the reality I may want to probably fail." This announcement well-known a deep-rooted fears of failure it's retaining you lower back from beginning your very own organization.

Another instance is probably a person who struggles with preserving relationships. Their finished sentence might be "I cannot keep relationships because of the truth humans continually end up leaving me." This declaration exposes a limiting belief that they'll be destined to be deserted, impacting their ability to form and preserve healthy relationships.

Similarly, assume you have been given commonly had a choice to travel the arena, however this dream stays unfulfilled. Applying the Fill-in-the-Blank method can also moreover result in a declaration like, "I can't adventure the place as it's now not constant," therefore revealing a limiting notion associated with the perceived risks of travelling, maintaining you from embarking on doubtlessly enriching adventures.

What makes the Fill-In-The-Blank method so powerful is its ability to offer shape to vague fears and uncertainties. By forcing you to articulate the motives in the back of your perceived incapability to acquire, be, or have a few factor you desire, it famous the fears you have got been hiding.

The human mind, with its super energy and have an impact on, serves as the architect of our realities. Our thoughts and ideals act due to the fact the blueprint, shaping our actions, attitudes, and ultimately, the place we enjoy. However, the complexity of this intellectual panorama is frequently underappreciated. Shockingly, studies from the National Science Foundation display that a thoughts-blowing eighty% of our mind are horrible, and possibly greater worryingly, ninety five% are repetitive (Simone, 2017) These unsettling records underscore the pivotal role of our concept methods in our lives. Often, we unknowingly act as our very private worst enemies, fortifying restricting beliefs that constrain our capacity and ward off our development.

The project, consequently, lies in locating a way out of this highbrow labyrinth through spotting our thoughts' electricity to create reality and harnessing this strength to foster private growth and well-being. We should trade the narrative in our minds from "I can't" to "I can" and "I will."

However, converting deeply entrenched ideals isn't always smooth. It's commonplace to stumble upon barriers together with worry of alternate, which includes resistance to new mind or views; confirmation bias, that is the tendency to interpret records based totally on our pre-modern ideals; and lack of self-focus, which makes it tough to grow to be privy to and undertaking horrible concept patterns and behaviors.

This bankruptcy explores strategies to conquer those limitations and ultimately, our proscribing ideals. Through this adventure, we'll project bad self-talk, use effective equipment like visualization, and promote a increase mind-set. The aim is to equip you with the statistics and equipment important to convert your mindset and, therefore, your lifestyles.

2A. POSITIVE SELF-TALK

The energy of language extends beyond the limits of interpersonal communiqué and shapes our intrapersonal communiqué, which is the continued communicate in our minds that considerably influences our perceptions and critiques of fact. This inner verbal exchange, frequently known as self-talk, is instrumental in shaping our beliefs and attitudes. Unfortunately, whilst left unchecked, it can come to be a breeding floor for terrible and proscribing ideals.

By consciously guidance this self-talk in a excellent path, we will substantially alter our highbrow panorama. Positive self-speak is far extra than most effective a cosmetic change of terms or forced positivity. It's a critical shift in the underlying beliefs that provide begin to our mind. When you deliberately engage in wonderful self-talk, you could counterbalance the horrible narrative that solidifies your restricting beliefs, changing it with a story of opportunity and functionality.

Positive self-communicate is a cornerstone of a boom mind-set—the belief that our abilities and intelligence can be honed and advanced via regular attempt and perseverance. If you adopt this mind-set, you can start viewing challenges no longer as insurmountable boundaries but as possibilities for increase and improvement.

Moreover, effective self-speak has numerous blessings: It fosters a more superb outlook, boosts self-self warranty, and enhances emotional resilience, thereby enhancing ordinary nicely-being. It furthermore enables manipulate stress, beautify typical overall performance, and keep a terrific attitude, even within the face of adversity.

Switching from terrible to high-quality self-communicate calls for a conscious strive and the utility of numerous key techniques.

The first method entails truth trying out, in which you determine the accuracy of your awful mind with the resource of manner of evaluating them to information. For example, in case you discover yourself thinking, "I commonly mess matters up," pause and don't forget the evidence. Have you in fact botched each undertaking you have undertaken, or are there instances of fulfillment that contradict this perception? More regularly than no longer, you could discover that your horrible self-talk is based on exaggerated perceptions and no longer real evidence. By project reality trying out, you can dispel those unfounded horrific ideals and update them with a greater correct and balanced view of your skills.

The second approach entails attempting to find opportunity elements or views that mission your horrible assumptions. You need to preserve in mind distinctive elements that in all likelihood contributed to a horrible final consequences and apprehend that it's miles natural for anyone to make mistakes and revel in setbacks when getting to know. Thus, you could shift your angle from a self-defeating outlook to considered one among studying and resilience.

The zero.33 technique is prepared putting subjects into mindset. Often, our terrible self-speak blows subjects out of percentage. However, thru stepping again and looking at the larger picture, you could gain a greater sensible mind-set. Ask yourself, "Will this depend in every week, a month, or twelve months?" Consider the capability consequences of your thoughts and moves. If you locate that yourself-speak is that specialize in insignificant subjects or worst-case eventualities which might be not going to seem, it's time to readjust your attitude to align with reality.

The closing method consists of adopting reason-directed thinking. Instead of ruminating over problems, you have to popularity on finding answers. Aim to choose out steps that can be taken to decorate any state of affairs, in desire to dwell at the negative components. For instance, in region of wondering, "I'm terrible at this," you might say, "I'm no longer as professional at this as I'd need to be but, but I can decorate with exercise and attempt."

Chapter 3: Behavioral Activation

Another powerful cognitive-behavioral approach is behavioral activation. This method is based totally mostly on the concept that our moves have an effect on our thoughts and emotions. It entails engaging in sports activities that evoke pleasure or a revel in of achievement, despite the fact that feeling unmotivated or terrible. These sports activities feature direct counterevidence to our limiting beliefs.

Behavioral activation helps disrupt the vicious cycle of horrible mind that result in state of being inactive or avoidance behaviors, which in flip, make more potent horrific mind. By pushing ourselves to engage in sports that supply pride or success, we generate new evidence that disturbing conditions our restricting ideals and allows reframe our terrible idea patterns at the identical time as boosting self warranty and self-efficacy.

Behavioral activation have to encompass easy sports like taking a stroll in nature, analyzing a book, working towards a hobby, or maybe finishing a small undertaking that has been pending for a while. The secret's to pick sports which can be meaningful and amusing. Over time, the feel of fulfillment and positivity derived from the ones sports activities can help overshadow terrible self-talk, promoting a extra high fine and proactive thoughts-set.

To beautify the effectiveness of behavioral activation, you must

1. Perceive sports activities which might be uniquely crucial to you.

2. Ensure the sports activities activities are precise and measurable.

3. List sports activities sports in order of problem.

Incorporating masses of activities can preserve the device attractive, and searching out assist from others can upload a layer of responsibility. Being aware during the ones sports sports, taking topics slowly, and profitable your development can also substantially bolster the effectiveness of behavioral activation.

Together, cognitive restructuring and behavioral activation offer a whole toolkit to task and reframe horrible thoughts, offering a powerful technique to transform your attitude and the way you understand yourself.

2C. HARNESSING VISUALIZATION TO OVERCOME LIMITING BELIEFS

The strength to exchange your mind-set and conquer restricting ideals moreover lies internal the suitable human functionality to visualize. Visualization, or highbrow imagery, is the machine of making compelling and vivid snap shots on your mind. This isn't a passive daydream, however as an opportunity an active engagement of the mind to assume carrying out a particular purpose or overcoming a specific undertaking.

The blessings of visualization are several and massive. Regular workout can motive expanded self-self guarantee, heightened motivation, and an greater perfect capability to recognition on your dreams. Furthermore, visualization can assist in lowering strain and selling general emotional nicely-being.

Visualization works to triumph over restricting beliefs thru using leveraging the brain's neuroplasticity, and capability to form and make stronger new neural pathways based totally mostly on experience and analyzing. When you time and again visualize fulfillment and excessive tremendous results, you basically educate your mind to accept as true with that you can reap those consequences. You create a new truth in your thoughts wherein success isn't most effective viable however also anticipated which leads to the arrival of new neural pathways that assist your newfound, empowering beliefs.

Implementing visualization consists of a sequence of cautiously taken into consideration steps.

Step 1: What Is Your Goal?

Firstly, you have to decide what you want to advantage or what undertaking you want to conquer. This workplace works the concept of your visualization and want to be some difficulty tremendous and in my opinion large.

Step 2: What Does It Look Like?

Once you have got diagnosed your aim, the subsequent step is to image it. Create an in depth intellectual image of the situation in which you bought your goal. Imagine the surroundings, the people gift, the sounds, the smells, and every The extra bright and unique your highbrow image, the more powerful your visualization might be.

Step 3: How Will You Reach It?

Next, maintain in thoughts the adventure within the direction of your success end. Visualize every step you need to take to advantage your intention. Feel the movements, the options, and the development for your visualization. This facilitates to create a revel in of realism and attainability to your thoughts.

Step four: What Will Achieving It Feel Like?

An crucial detail of visualization is replicating the emotion you'll sense on conducting your aim. This facilitates to cement the perception on your mind that your purpose is inner accumulate. It's about experiencing the delight, pride, comfort, or any of the opportunity first-rate feelings associated with your success.

Remember, for visualization to be effective, it want to be a regular exercise. Set aside time for it every day. Consistency is the key to reinforcing your new ideals and making them an important a part of your mind-set. To maximize the effectiveness of visualization, preserve in thoughts the subsequent pointers.

Choose quiet surroundings unfastened from distractions.

Invoke all your senses to make intellectual imagery extra sensible and attractive.

Always visualize from a number one-man or woman angle—see the motion unfold through your non-public eyes, no longer as a indifferent observer.

Write down your visualization research to hold song of your development and refine your exercising.

2D. POSITIVE AFFIRMATIONS

Positive affirmations are effective system to modify one's outlook. They are quick, upbeat statements supposed to replace horrific techniques of questioning and shape your attitudes and actions. Consistent use of such affirmations has been established to modify one's way of thinking over time, essential to an increase in optimism and self-guarantee. These excellent statements have the electricity to little by little update limiting ideals, increase one's scope of opportunity, and unencumbered one's complete capacity.

The terrible proscribing ideals that stand in the manner of your achievement may be at once faced and countered via exquisite affirmations. By replacing your ingrained bad narratives with exceptional empowering beliefs, your subconscious may be reprogrammed through the each day exercise of quality affirmations. It is the combination of these assertions with the purpose or treatment to act that produces the effects.

Affirmations are grounded in our expertise of neuroplasticity. When repeated often, immoderate best affirmations were established to adjust the shape of neural networks within the thoughts and because of this one's manner of questioning and perceiving the sector round them.

To illustrate the power of tremendous affirmations, don't forget the following: "I am capable and strong, and I can deal with any undertaking that comes my way." Another possible confirmation is, "I want to gain success, loved, and happy." Positive self-photograph and self belief in a single's very own capabilities is the cornerstones of success.

Several hints may be observed to increase the performance of excessive quality affirmations.

Rule 1: Affirmations have to be written within the present annoying as although the final outcomes being sought were already the case. As an opportunity to "I is probably a fulfillment," you could say "I am a hit." This makes it easier in your brain to in reality take delivery of the desired state because the modern-day-day one.

Rule 2: Affirmations need to be actual and diploma-headed in reality. To cause them to impactful and achievable, they need to mirror practical desires or beliefs which you keep high-priced.

Rule three: Affirmations should be practiced every day to perform their true ability. Repetition is the essential aspect to absolutely setting up the ones beliefs on your thoughts.

Rule 4: Affirmations ought to be written within the first character. This makes them greater specific to you, which will increase their danger of getting an impact for your unconscious mind. An illustrative assertion will be, "I am resilient and may conquer any impediment."

Rule five: Affirmations have to be associated with an emotion or movement they may be meant to inspire. When you are pronouncing a few element like "I am calm and centered," as an instance, cause to in fact revel in non violent and balanced. Making an emotional reference to the affirmation makes it more effective in terms of bringing about a shift in mind-set.

3:REWIRING YOUR BRAIN

As we begin this bankruptcy, the terms of the Buddha, an historical decide whose teachings have inspired cultures and people international, set a becoming tone. It isn't always uncommon for us to fall into wondering patterns that limit our functionality or leave us feeling unworthy. This bankruptcy is devoted to statistics neuroplasticity, a modern idea that offers a scientific basis to the Buddha's knowledge and holds the key to liberating ourselves from restricting ideals.

3A. STRESS, NEGATIVITY, AND THEIR EFFECTS ON THE BRAIN

The mechanics of rewiring our thoughts hinge upon information the consequences of pervasive factors inclusive of stress and negativity. Stress, especially, impacts vital regions of the mind such as the hippocampus, which manages reading and reminiscence. As Kim et al. (2015) determined, extended durations of stress can decrease hippocampal amount, impairing memory and mastering capabilities. In a running expert's existence, persistent pressure also can motive problem in absorbing new information, remembering responsibilities, or maybe analyzing new capabilities. Additionally, strain pushes the thoughts to revert to ingrained types of conduct, often reinforcing restricting ideals and terrible concept styles, a survival instinct no longer in particular useful in nowadays's global.

Exploring the Vicious Cycle of Negativity

The impact of negativity is full-size usually due to the vicious cycle it establishes with pressure. The thoughts's propensity toward negativity biases can reason strain, further fueling negativity and establishing a self-feeding loop (Baumeister et al., 2001). For instance, even a chunk horrible remarks at paintings can also moreover moreover cloud our perception, causing us to overlook the numerous first rate remarks we get preserve of. This can bring about stress, which then leads us to anticipate extra poor testimonies, consequently forming a cycle. Consequently, breaking this cycle thru conscious effort and positivity is prime inside the use of neuroplasticity to reshape our minds.

The Connection Between Stress, Negativity, and Emotional Regulation

We want to understand the impact of pressure and negativity on our thoughts's prefrontal areas, which may be answerable for functions like choice-making and emotional regulation. Stress and negativity can disrupt connectivity between the dorsal and ventral prefrontal areas, affecting our capability to regulate emotions successfully (Morawetz et al., 2016). For instance, underneath the impact of extended pressure, we'd react extra all of a sudden or struggle to control our emotions on the equal time as confronted with challenges.

Leveraging Neuroplasticity to Overcome Stress and Negativity

Comprehending the impact of stress and negativity is the first step to leveraging neuroplasticity, because it lets in us emerge as aware of and assignment our unfavourable styles. Our neural networks are inspired with the beneficial aid of our critiques and intellectual states. Therefore, regular pressure and negativity could make more potent pathways related to anxiety, worry, and restricting beliefs, therefore making it an increasing number of hard to interrupt far from those negative concept patterns (Davidson & McEwen, 2012).

Strategies to Combat Stress and Negativity

Armed with expertise approximately the outcomes of strain and negativity, we are able to increase techniques to combat detrimental idea patterns. Techniques to manipulate strain successfully, like mindfulness and cognitive-behavioral techniques, can assist us reframe our horrific thoughts into extra positive ones. To reduce strain degrees, recollect schooling mindfulness and specializing in the present to decrease rumination over past terrible opinions or issues about the future. Furthermore, consciously choosing positivity can rebalance our brain's negativity bias, fostering a balanced perspective that helps our journey closer to overcoming limiting beliefs.

Understanding the results of strain and negativity presents us with the critical records to stand those disturbing situations head-on. As such, we can begin to recognize the patterns that pressure and negativity perpetuate in our lives and prepare to break loose from them.

3B. UNRAVELING THE CONCEPT OF NEUROPLASTICITY

Neuroplasticity, in essence, is the thoughts's capability to rewire itself. It refers back to the physical changes that get up inside the mind in response to reading, revel in, or harm. In a sensible enjoy, neuroplasticity method that we very personal the functionality to reframe our thoughts's wiring, fostering smooth types of wondering, feeling, and behaving. This capability is our most strong weapon in opposition to the restrictive confines of limiting ideals.

Research has indicated that our movements, thoughts, and emotions can bodily regulate the thoughts's structure and function (Dayan

& Cohen, 2011). This manner that outstanding thoughts and behaviors, together with walking toward mindfulness, can make more potent neural networks related to happiness, resilience, and self-self belief, providing us a profound manner to transform our lives from the internal out.

Neuroplasticity additionally offers a charming angle on our functionality to change. It puts forth the empowering message that we are not doomed to copy patterns of behavior that restriction our increase. This concept proper now contradicts the previous belief that our character trends and behaviors cannot exchange past a nice age, in addition reinforcing the truth that exchange is feasible at any degree of life (Dayan & Cohen, 2011).

Chapter 4: Practical Strategies to Leverage Neuro Plasticity

Harnessing the strength of neuro plasticity calls for conscious and everyday efforts these efforts comprise conduct that promotes highbrow properly-being, along with aware meditation, physical exercising, and positivity.

Mindful meditation is a powerful device that promotes neuroplasticity. It encourages us to consciousness at the prevailing, which extensively reduces stress and tension stages, the commonplace culprits within the lower returned of restricting beliefs. Practicing mindfulness engages one-of-a-kind regions of our brains, fostering new neural pathways.

Physical exercising enables neuroplasticity through enhancing the overall health of our brains. Regular bodily hobby can create new neural connections and bring about superior mental sturdiness and resilience, which might be essentlal for overcoming proscribing beliefs.

Positivity is vital to create the suitable surroundings for neuroplasticity optimization. Our brains generally tend to pay extra hobby to terrible studies, so deliberately that specialize in high pleasant research can counteract this bias and rewire our brains to growth effective mind and emotions.

Neuroplasticity plays an crucial function in fortifying the neural connections we regularly rent at the same time as diminishing the hardly ever used ones.

The Integral Role of Environment and Lifestyle in Neuroplasticity: Designing a Neurologically Nurturing Atmosphere

The settings wherein we find out ourselves and the manner of existence alternatives we make have a large effect on our brains' abilties to comply and change in reaction to reminiscences. The surroundings and the way of lifestyles we adhere to are two of the most effective influencers on this equation.

To located it really, our brains flourish even as they'll be exposed to environments that abound with novelty and highbrow stimulation. These might in all likelihood encompass interactive opinions, progressive hobbies, instructional possibilities, or maybe exploring new physical landscapes. Each of these gives a wealthy tapestry of sensory and cognitive stimuli that the mind will have interaction with, encouraging the formation of latest neural connections, and therefore improving neuroplasticity. Additionally, additionally they serve to beautify cognitive feature and sell clarity of concept, creativity, and hassle-fixing skills.

That said, correct sufficient relaxation and sleep are further critical for brain fitness. As you sleep, your body and mind heal and rejuvenate. The mind, mainly, consolidates memories, methods the day's reports, and detoxifies dangerous waste merchandise in this time. Thus, loss of good enough sleep can severely impair neuroplasticity and cognitive general performance, similarly solidifying the importance of preserving proper sleep hygiene and ensuring enough rest to assist the thoughts's adaptive tactics.

Awareness: The Prelude to Personal Transformation

Every adventure starts offevolved with a unmarried step, and in the quest for cognitive alternate, step one is focus. Awareness entails introspecting and identifying restricting beliefs and terrible concept patterns that, whilst often subtle, exert big impact over your existence.

This journey of self-discovery is a long way from sincere. It calls for a robust strength of will to self-focus and the braveness to confront the unknown components of yourself. You ought to peel once more layers of observed behaviors and everyday wondering patterns to show the underlying structures that form your perceptions of yourself and the location round you.

Reframing: Charting a New Course for Mental Narratives

Once reputation is installation, the subsequent step is reframing. Here, we deliberately update our restricting ideals and negative perception styles with folks who promote increase and self-efficacy. The motive isn't always simply to adopt a powerful mindset but as an alternative to foster sensible and permitting mind that align with our center values and lifestyles dreams.

Now comes the tough part of making adjustments. You have to mission long-held ideals, query ingrained assumptions, and actively choose thoughts that better serve your aspirations. It's all approximately rewriting the narrative of your inner global and crafting a highbrow panorama that encourages private growth, resilience, and success.

Reinforcement: Solidifying New Pathways for Empowered Thinking

The final segment in leveraging neuroplasticity is reinforcement. This includes actively attractive with the modern day, empowering narratives and integrating them into your each day mind and movements until they come to be 2d nature. Remember, your thoughts strengthens new connections and weakens antique ones through repetition, so you want to be disciplined and steadfast.

Unleashing the Power of Neuroplasticity: Translating Theory Into Practice

Through the ordinary application of these steps, we are able to tap into the transformative ability of neuroplasticity. When we deliberately choose extra healthy, more beneficial concept patterns and beef up them through repetition, we purpose them to the identical vintage framework of our cognitive approaches.

As such, we flip precept into exercise, utilising the inherent flexibility of our brains to decorate our wonderful of existence. Neuroplasticity has the fantastic strength to trade our brains, and as a result ourselves, for the better. Through cognizance, reframing, and reinforcement, we are capable of break free from proscribing beliefs and foster a mind-set that allows boom, empowerment, and personal success.

3C. MINDFULNESS AND ITS TRANSFORMATIVE POWER

Mindfulness has the capability to purpose a massive growth in close by brain grey rely density. This trade is predominantly massive in structures crucial to mastering, memory strategies, emotional regulation, self-referential processing, and mind-set-taking. In essence, everyday mindfulness workout can effectively reshape your thoughts, enhancing its efficiency in processing data and managing emotions. In a global that frequently feels chaotic and overwhelming, such adjustments can result in profound advantages like advanced emotional manage, heightened cognizance, and a more sense of well-being.

Mindfulness: Fostering Emotional Regulation

At its center, mindfulness introduces a experience of objectivity in the direction of our thoughts and emotions. Instead of being engulfed in a whirlwind of emotional reactions, we're advocated to apprehend our thoughts and emotions as brief sports. Such a change in mind-set empowers us to reply to critiques in desire to to unexpectedly react to them. This self-law, driven with the aid of mindfulness, might be attributed to changes in mind networks associated with self-control (Tang et al., 2015).

3-d. KEY TAKEAWAYS

In this monetary break, we've mentioned the significance of neuroplasticity, our brain's incredible functionality to alternate and adapt, and its vital function in non-public increase. Understanding the formation and reinforcement of neural pathways offers insight into the demanding situations and opportunities related to converting limiting beliefs.

Mindfulness practices like conscious respiration, meditation, frame test, conscious movement, and aware consuming have been studied as effective equipment for converting our thoughts's wiring and selling more wholesome mind and behaviors. Each of those practices improves self-reputation, emotional regulation, and neuroplasticity, as a cease result supporting in the alternative of limiting ideals with empowering ones.

4A. THE PARALYSIS OF OVERTHINKING

Life in its specially complex nature, often offers us with an problematic dance of mind. It's a commonplace revel in to find out ourselves out of vicinity in a whirl of contemplations about our beyond, gift, and destiny. While thinking about about lifestyles may be insightful, there's a factor in which it will become excessive and results in overthinking.

Overthinking, characterised by way of way of way of persistent worrying and 2nd-guessing choices, often outcomes in 'assessment paralysis' in which human beings find out it hard to make alternatives because of immoderate contemplation. It can present various signs and symptoms and signs and symptoms:

Mental exhaustion from non-forestall ruminating mind.

All-or-no longer something thinking that ends in pressure and ignored possibilities.

Catastrophizing or seeking out worst-case conditions.

Overgeneralizing past terrible opinions while studying future activities.

Overthinking can be a natural response to stress or uncertainty, but it is able to additionally suggest anxiety, despair, or unique intellectual health issues. It can result in bad idea styles, stepped forward anxiety and fear, problems making picks, and reduced trouble-solving capability.

4B. THE ROOT CAUSES OF OVERTHINKING

Navigating our minds' large landscapes regularly reveals paths that reason overthinking, a mental phenomenon that binds and bewilders many. Identifying its root reasons is much like unraveling a complicated puzzle, which on crowning glory will offer notion into why the thoughts every now and then spirals into ceaseless contemplation. That stated, the reasons for overthinking are multifaceted and interwoven, developing a tapestry of highbrow worrying situations. Here are some root causes that you could pick out out with.

Not Being Solution-Oriented: This mind-set, lost in problems in desire to capability solutions, serves as fertile ground for overthinking, breeding a cycle of stagnation and worry. When you're now not centered on locating a manner to a hassle, your mind can hold cycling through the equal thoughts without making any development.

Experiencing Repetitive Thoughts: Like echoes in a canyon, repetitive mind soar and reverberate within the thoughts, growing a constant loop that traps you in a nation of intellectual restlessness. This is specifically right if the mind are terrible or cause fear.

Inability to Quiet Your Mind: A thoughts that refuses to quiet will become a continual noise, drowning out readability and recognition and turning the symphony of mind into cacophony. One motive your mind can be unable to close off is due to an imbalance within the neurotransmitters that modify mood and cognitive function. Additionally, persistent stress and tension can purpose an overactive amygdala, that may make it tough to reveal off horrible mind and emotions.

Struggling to Decide: When each preference turns into a struggle, the warfare to decide amplifies doubt and lack of confidence, feeding the beast of overthinking. There might be many reasons why you battle with decision-making—fear of creating the incorrect selection, being indecisive, or outdoor pressures and expectations.

Second-Guessing Decisions: The shadow of doubt that follows choices can turn self assurance into uncertainty, most vital to a by no means-finishing cycle of questioning and reevaluation.

Understanding these root motives of overthinking is a important step in the adventure to intellectual clarity, and it permits you untangle your internet of mind and steer your mind in the direction of tranquility and reason.

4C. THE MANY FACES OF OVERTHINKING

The signs and symptoms and symptoms and signs of overthinking are as numerous because the folks who enjoy them. Some people discover themselves wrestling with the identical thoughts or concerns for hours on give up. Others constantly 2nd-bet their selections, in no way feeling confident or satisfied with the picks they make. An insidious shape of exhaustion comes with overthinking that could feel like your brain might not transfer off, even at the same time as you desperately want it to.

More concerningly, overthinking also can result in all-or-nothing questioning, catastrophizing, overgeneralizing, or ruminating at the beyond.

All or Nothing

All-or-no longer some thing questioning traps us in a global of absolutes in which topics are each perfect or a catastrophe. Such thinking is regularly associated with perfectionism and may reason strain, anxiety, and overlooked possibilities. For example, you may think that during case you don't get pinnacle rankings on a take a look at, you're a failure or if you may't play piano like Beethoven, you shouldn't play in any respect. Black or white questioning like this hinders non-public boom and is poisonous to the mind.

Catastrophizing

Here, we exaggerate issues and prepare for the worst. It's like having an annoying stone to your shoe but wondering you will lose your foot. Such questioning is frequently connected to anxiety issues and might intrude with trouble-solving and desire-making talents (American Psychological Association, 2021). For example, when you have a slight quarrel with a friend, you might imagine that your friendship has been irreversibly harmed. Overthinking like this may result in feelings of depression and hopelessness, making it now not possible to move on.

Overgeneralizing

When we observe one horrible revel in to all future ones, we overgeneralize. We count on that if we've failed as quickly as, we'll fail every time. This can restrict our willingness to take risks and undermine our self-self perception. For example, in case you've taken a cause force's take a look at as quickly as and failed or in case you've caused a small twist of fate whilst analyzing, you'll preserve going decrease again to that experience and revel in like using isn't meant for you and which you want to provide it up.

Ruminating

Ruminating on the past can tie us to our antique mistakes and regrets, preventing us from playing the prevailing and securing a notable future. For example, when you have a terrible process interview enjoy, you could start to count on that you could never be able to get a notable pastime and that you are unqualified for any characteristic you may choice. This may want to make you sense defeated and restriction your motivation.

Research suggests that overthinkers generally tend to have greater stress, revel in better tiers of tension and despair, and conflict with sleep issues (Wilding, 2021). It's a dependancy that not great reasons emotional distress however additionally has severe implications for fitness.

4D. THE ROAD TO QUIETING YOUR MIND

Let's unpack this treasure trove of tips and strategies that reduce overthinking. Overthinking isn't always a lifelong settlement you're caught with. It's high-quality a dependancy, and behavior may be modified. There's a whole toolbox of techniques and strategies to help you in your journey.

Set Up Worry Periods

One powerful method is putting in a fear length (Healthline, 2021). Sounds awesome, does no longer it? But it's far like scheduling an appointment together together with your problems. During this unique time each day, you allow your self to worry, to allow those mind run wild. However, outside of this period, you educate your thoughts to stay clean of these intrusive thoughts. The trick right proper right here is compartmentalizing your issues, giving them a selected time and vicinity, and no longer letting them invade the rest of your day.

Chapter 5: Challenge Negative Thoughts

Another technique includes tough the ones bad mind and thinking the "what ifs" that regularly gas overthinking (Cuncic, 2020). You're not denying your problems but as a substitute confronting them and asking, "Is this worry rational? How likely is it to show up?" This approach encourages a greater balanced angle, assisting to lower the impact of overthinking on your emotions and behaviors.

Distract Yourself

Distracting yourself with hobbies or physical sports activities is likewise a treasured technique (Healthline, 2021). Imagine your brain as a laptop with multiple tabs open. A interest may be a latest, interesting tab that diverts interest from the priority tab. Hobbies help us stay inside the second, and thru engaging our brains in a completely unique, enjoyable way, they go away little room for rumination. Exercise offers twin blessings. Besides the distraction, it moreover releases endorphins, our frame's natural mood elevators, which can help counteract the stress and tension associated with overthinking.

Practice Mindfulness

Mindfulness practices, which encompass meditation, are also beneficial (Cleveland Clinic, 2021). They assist you emerge as greater aware of your thoughts and feelings and have a look at them with out getting entangled in them. It's like watching a movie with out getting absorbed in the tale. This interest can lessen the electricity of overthinking, offering you with in choice to your thoughts manage.

Stay inside the Now

Grounding yourself within the gift and genuinely immersing your self in a few element you are doing right now is some different beneficial tool. It's about being right right here and now without thinking about what has came about or what will take place.

Additionally, schooling self-compassion, forgiveness, and gratitude can shift your attitude, lowering the effect of horrible self-communicate and enhancing your conventional nicely-being.

4E. JOURNAL YOUR WAY THROUGH

Now, we'll speak approximately some self-compassion mag turns on. These are guided questions or statements in order to can help you write reflectively approximately your mind and emotions. For instance, a prompt is probably, "Write about a time you felt misunderstood. How are you capable to reveal kindness to yourself for the duration of such moments?" These turns on guide you toward knowledge and accepting your emotions, supplying you a slight way to discover and navigate your emotional panorama. By penning your thoughts and emotions, you no longer handiest advantage a deeper information of yourself, but you moreover mght create a stable location to manner your stories, which can be an effective device in overcoming overthinking.

So, at the same time as the journey could in all likelihood appear tough, consider that you've had been given an arsenal of techniques and techniques to manual you. Overthinking is probably a addiction, however it does not define you, and most importantly, it is a dependancy that can be damaged.

Start through the usage of a number of those phrases to be kinder to your self. Think approximately them and write approximately your impressions and the manner each phrase makes you experience.

1. It's adequate that I experience a high-quality way.

2. This enjoy will help me expand.

3. It's ok that a situation is hard due to the truth I will discover my manner thru it.

4. I'll study this example from unique views before I react.

5.   I'm no longer my thoughts.

Once you spend a while with these terms and notable affirmations and write your reactions, try some of the ones magazine activates to in reality find out the ideas.

1.   What can you take from your routine on the manner to make your days happier? Will eliminating this item provide you with time for self-care?

2.   What is one expectation that makes you experience compelled in existence?

3.   What pressure are you currently managing? What advice might you offer a friend who become handling the equal hassle? Give that recommendation to yourself with kindness.

four.   What vicinity of life feels maximum chaotic to you and why? Are there procedures you can become greater organized in this realm?

five. What is a few issue presently disappointing you to your life? Do you have got the electricity to alternate it? Write down three methods you could turn your disappointment proper proper into a aspect of fulfillment and productivity.

After answering those questions, reflect on how your mindset has changed. Do you revel in like you are extra remarkable common? Do you get preserve of others as they will be? Do you provide your self extra grace? The ordinary intention of this interactive workout need to be to enjoy self-compassion. This exceptional, in flip, will assist you revel in kinder towards genuinely everyone in the international spherical you and help you boom a great outlook in lifestyles.

5UNLEASH YOUR INNER WARRIOR

Mental sturdiness is greater important than you may accept as actual with. Think of the last few years, with the pandemic, social upheaval, financial issues, and considered one of a kind matters you can by no means have expected to face. Making it thru the ones boundaries calls for resilience and grit. If you feel inclusive of you're suffering and aren't able to those feats, in no manner worry—you can empower your inner warrior.

5A. UNDERSTANDING MENTAL TOUGHNESS

The quest for private growth and dismantling restricting beliefs calls for a guiding celebrity: intellectual sturdiness. This complex trait, frequently misconstrued as mere resilience, is a powerful mixture of numerous highbrow competencies. It empowers us to cope with immoderate-stakes needs, navigate adversity, and continuously supply peak performance (Jones et al., 2007).

At the heart of intellectual toughness lie numerous core elements:

Emotional Regulation: Allows you to keep emotional stability in annoying conditions.

Optimism: Helps you hold a super outlook amidst setbacks.

Self-Belief: Fuels yourself assurance and conviction in your competencies.

Together, the ones tendencies forge the resilient framework of highbrow sturdiness, preparing you to meet demanding conditions head-on.

Embracing your inner warrior calls so that it will draw to your internal reserves of energy and perseverance by way of developing self-warranty, assertiveness, and a treatment to overcome issues and benefit personal desires. Moreover, it requires you to simply accept vulnerability, confront fears, and take a look at from setbacks.

The Transformative Power of Mental Toughness

Why does mental toughness play a pivotal feature in breaking free from limiting beliefs? The efficiency of this trait lies in its transformative effects on yourself-notion and approach to adversity and lifestyles in ultra-modern.

Mental longevity acts as a catalyst for maintaining high-degree performance, even amidst stress and strain (Gucciardi et al., 2012). It permits you navigate lifestyles's inevitable obstacles at the identical time as fostering a robust belief in your self, propelling you in the direction of your desires.

As you cultivate this trait, you dismantle fear, self-doubt, and limiting beliefs, paving the manner for bravery, conviction, and an indomitable spirit.

Research affirms the numerous blessings of intellectual sturdiness (Crust & Clough, 2005):

Enhanced pressure manipulate

Improved awareness

Sustained high ordinary common overall performance beneath stress

These factors are important in putting off limiting ideals, as a result underscoring the important role of highbrow sturdiness in non-public increase.

Chapter 6: Mental Toughness in Action

As we adventure in the direction of cultivating intellectual sturdiness, reading real-existence case studies can offer treasured insights. The studies of those who have walked this path remove darkness from the transformative energy of intellectual sturdiness in surmounting self-imposed boundaries.

Mental durability is going beyond commonplace misconceptions of being a trifling synonym for resilience or grit. It is, in truth, a complicated weave of mental capabilities and attributes. The narrative of pinnacle-tier athletes or corporate leaders who thrive underneath stress illustrates how this trait isn't always restrained to physical abilities or strategic prowess by myself, however closely leans on intellectual durability.

Mental Toughness: Not Just for the Elite

Contrary to the belief that highbrow durability is reserved for excessive achievers, it's far an adaptable trait available to each person (Gucciardi et al., 2012). Regardless of your past or present conditions, highbrow sturdiness may be intentionally honed and bolstered, empowering you to navigate stress and adversity successfully.

Mental sturdiness affects the way you manage adversity and understand yourself and shapes your existence's path. This intellectual fortitude enables you to feature below stress, grapple with demanding situations, and foster an unshakeable belief in your abilties. Your beyond reports or cutting-edge situations do now not outline your potential to cultivate highbrow sturdiness; it is a understanding that can be consciously advanced and strengthened.

Now, permit's dive deeper into why intellectual toughness is pivotal for overcoming limiting beliefs. In essence, mental sturdiness primes you for personal growth, freeing you from the restrictions of proscribing beliefs. It equips you with a resilient thoughts-set, allowing you to technique existence with braveness and conviction, transitioning you from a reactionary being to a proactive architect of your lifestyles.

On unraveling the components of mental sturdiness, we come across resilience, optimism, emotional manage, and self-notion as key additives.

Resilience lets in you to recover from setbacks, viewing disasters as growth opportunities instead of roadblocks. Optimism permits preserve a nice outlook, treating challenges as short hurdles. Emotional manage lets you control your emotional responses successfully, maintaining composure below strain. Lastly, self-belief, the unwavering conviction on your talents, propels you via self-doubt and fear, critical you closer to your preferred consequences.

Mental sturdiness is a quit result of those and different additives, forming a intellectual armor safeguarding us from the negative affects of strain, adversity, and failure.

The Four Cs of Mental Toughness

Let's dive into the crux of mental sturdiness, that is widely categorised into 4 foremost additives: manipulate, commitment, project, and self warranty. Each of those additives is instrumental to your journey to move beyond restricting beliefs.

Control

Control refers to the capability to regulate your mind, feelings, and events efficiently. For instance, an govt dealing with a important undertaking beneath tight last dates famous manipulate once they balance the team's stress tiers even as steering the project inside the right direction.

Practical Tip: Incorporate practices like mindfulness, which enhances emotional regulation and energy of thoughts.

Commitment

Commitment, the subsequent element, displays your willpower to paste in your desires, however the hurdles that come your way. Think of an athlete who, no matter an harm, stays dedicated to their restoration and returns to the game.

Practical Tip: Foster dedication using the SMART (Specific, Measurable, Achievable, Relevant, Time-nice) cause-putting approach that promotes readability and electricity of mind.

Challenge

Challenge is all approximately the way you recognize troubles. Those with a immoderate level of intellectual sturdiness welcome stressful conditions, the usage of them as stepping stones towards their goals. A budding entrepreneur, for example, may want to in all likelihood view the release of a competitive product as a challenge to improve their personal.

Practical Tip: To beautify this trait, adopt a growth mind-set that sees annoying conditions as possibilities.

Confidence

Lastly, your unwavering faith on your very private abilties is the bedrock on which self assure rests. Consider the self-assuredness of a pro musician about to step onto a stage within the the front of hundreds of enthusiasts.

Practical Tip: Bolster self assure through self-affirmation physical sports and thru reframing your self-notion definitely.

The Role of Emotional Intelligence in Mental Toughness

Emotional intelligence illuminates the crucial interaction amongst emotional acuity and highbrow durability. This connection encompasses the notion, comprehension, manipulate, and alertness of emotions with emotional intelligence serving as an engine propelling mental sturdiness.

Self-Awareness: The First Step

Self-recognition, or the aware recognition and know-how of 1's emotions, is a cornerstone of emotional intelligence. This vital detail facilitates you apprehend how your feelings form your mind, alternatives, and actions. Heightened self-consciousness maintains feelings from using your options off path, allowing you to find out them, understand their origins, and weigh their effect in advance than deciding on your subsequent step.

Consider a immoderate-stakes poker participant, as an instance. With self-awareness, they recognize their anxiety, recognize its roots, and might channel this strength into keeping a keen popularity, turning what can be a quandary into an advantage.

Emotional Regulation: The Steering Wheel

Emotional regulation refers to our capability to manipulate emotions in keeping with our goals and the current state of affairs. This capabilities carefully ties into the manipulate detail of intellectual durability. For instance, an entrepreneur weathering the disintegrate of a venture also can modify feelings to govern disappointment constructively, preserve recognition, and find out the resilience to start over, embodying intellectual sturdiness.

Laborde et al.'s (2016) research confirms the connection among emotional intelligence and mental durability. Higher emotional intelligence equates to multiplied highbrow sturdiness, way to 1's capability to recognize, control, and use one's feelings effectively and foster resilience in the face of adversity.

Empathy: Connecting With Others

Understanding empathy, a center aspect of emotional intelligence, proves useful for intellectual durability. Empathy no longer only lets in you recognise others' emotions but additionally bolsters interpersonal relationships, establishing a assist network that fosters emotional resilience in tough instances. A group chief who practices empathy, as an instance, can higher maintain close the emotional states of group members, fostering a supportive and cohesive work environment, as a end result developing the institution's resilience.

Leveraging Emotions to Facilitate Thought

Emotional intelligence offers the capacity to leverage feelings to facilitate perception, it is essential for intellectual sturdiness. Emotions serve twin roles—they're responses to events and drivers of cognitive strategies (Damasio, 1994). Harnessing feelings to guide your thinking integrates emotional responses into cognitive techniques, enhancing your capacity to navigate stressful situations and make sound alternatives.

For example, an crook expert engaged in a high-stress court docket docket case may additionally additionally leverage their anxiety to put together more comprehensively, transforming worry into proactive motion.

To domesticate emotional intelligence, you need to be aware about your emotional nation and remember it as precious notion. Treating emotions as informative data better equips you to persuade your alternatives and movements, in location of being swayed through emotional responses.

Resilience: Turning Adversity into Advantage

Resilience is the cornerstone of highbrow sturdiness. It is the paintings of adapting virtually to adversity, trauma, threats, or giant strain. The motive is not to keep away from stress but as an alternative to learn how to thrive with it.

To foster resilience, developing a pleasant outlook is crucial. Positive emotions counterbalance the results of pressure and foster quicker healing (Fredrickson, 2001). You can work out positivity thru

actively searching out glad factors on your life.

retaining a gratitude magazine to habituate positivity.

Consider a firefighter who faces danger each day. They foster resilience by using finding joy inside the a hit execution in their task and gratitude for the lives they save.

Growth Mindset: Learning within the Face of Challenges

A increase mind-set is a few different sturdy technique to construct intellectual sturdiness. It includes viewing disturbing conditions as opportunities for gaining knowledge of instead of threats and embracing the functionality for growth and improvement.

To cultivate a growth mind-set, self-attention approximately your self-communicate and notion gadget is important. Challenging self-defeating thoughts and reframing them clearly fosters a increase attitude. A scholar struggling with complex math problems, for instance, can shift from feeling defeated to seeing the situation as an possibility to look at and broaden.

Chapter 7: Mastering Your Response

Stress management is essential to building highbrow durability. You can manage pressure with the useful resource of changing the annoying scenario, converting your response to the state of affairs, or finding strategies to take care of your emotional and bodily health. Proven strategies encompass deep respiratory, mindfulness, yoga, and everyday exercising (Chen et al., 2015).

Living With Purpose: Aligning Actions With Values

A cause in existence, or a smooth understanding of what in fact topics to you, is a giant predictor of highbrow sturdiness. Identifying your passion and what you're inclined to war for can help align your moves together with your values, thereby improving highbrow durability. For example, a social employee can also additionally face emotional pressure, but their clean purpose of helping others keeps them mentally tough.

The Benefits of Mental Toughness

Boosting overall performance is one of the many benefits of highbrow durability, as strengthened thru an intensive evaluation by means of manner of Gucciardi et al. (2015). They scrutinized studies from sports activities sports, enterprise, and educational arenas, all pointing in the direction of a awesome courting among highbrow durability and everyday performance results. Whether you are assembly a lessen-off date at art work, striving for instructional excellence, or aspiring for athletic triumphs, mental sturdiness fuels success. It furnishes the intellectual staying power had to keep hobby, overcome hurdles, and rebound from setbacks. This intellectual robustness guarantees pinnacle of the road standard performance, irrespective of the adversities confronted.

Stress Resilience: A Byproduct of Mental Toughness

Research thru way of Siddle et al. (2009) underscores the importance of highbrow durability in managing pressure. Those with better levels of highbrow durability interpret traumatic conditions as a whole lot less threatening, exerting extra control over their responses. These human beings hold their poise, making effective selections no matter the pressure they face. In a international in which strain is a regular associate, intellectual toughness bestows you with the abilties to govern, thereby selling highbrow health and regularly going on nicely-being.

Overcoming Limiting Beliefs Through Mental Toughness

Crust and Azadi (2010) highlight the correlation amongst intellectual sturdiness and the capability to undertaking self-imposed obstacles. Individuals with excessive intellectual durability harness first-rate cognitive techniques, which includes advantageous self-communicate and visualization, to break loose from the shackles of self-doubt. Instead of being deterred via the fear of failure, they recognize boundaries as boom possibilities. Essentially, intellectual toughness erects a mental defend in competition to proscribing beliefs, releasing people to faucet into their complete ability.

Emotional Intelligence and Self-Belief: The Extended Benefits of Mental Toughness

Apart from improving overall performance and coping with strain, intellectual durability contributes to effective private and interpersonal dynamics. It reinforces thoughts of emotional intelligence, fostering an unshakeable feel of self-belief. These attributes, in flip, can increase regular existence delight and enhance relationships, stimulating a cycle of persevered private increase.

Resilience, a cornerstone of highbrow durability, equips people to navigate lifestyles's vicissitudes more efficaciously. They remain calm in a few unspecified time within the destiny of crises, seeing stressful situations as transitory hurdles in preference to impassable barriers. This perspective fosters proactive problem-solving in place of denial or avoidance. It offers people the braveness to confront troubles and the resilience to get over setbacks.

The impact of intellectual longevity on interpersonal relationships cannot be unnoticed. Those with excessive highbrow longevity display off emotional manage, primary to superior communication and empathy. They manipulate complicated conversations with out dropping their cool and empathize with out being beaten with the useful resource of feelings. This capability paves the manner for powerful communication, battle decision, and stronger relationships.

Mental sturdiness moreover offers beginning to a strong feel of self-belief. Mentally hard humans very own corporation faith in their abilties and the self notion to chase their desires, unswayed via using outside judgment. This self-assure is a ways from arrogance; it is a grounded belief in their capability, intertwined with the information that there may be constantly room for growth. This aggregate of self-belief and humility fosters a non-stop choice for self-development, steering individuals toward non-public and expert milestones.

5B. CASE STUDIES OF MENTAL TOUGHNESS

Malala Yousafzai: Beacon of Resilience and Advocacy

At the coronary heart of our exploration of intellectual durability is Malala Yousafzai. As a younger woman, she stood in competition to the Taliban, advocating for women' schooling in Pakistan. She confirmed excellent braveness and resilience, surviving an assassination try and leveraging her international platform to maintain her advocacy. Yousafzai's profound announcement, "One infant, one trainer, one ebook, one pen can change the sector," is a testomony to her unyielding spirit. Her adventure epitomizes the power of resilience and courage amidst excessive adversity.

Serena Williams: Testament for Resilience in Sports

Transitioning to the sports activities sports arena, we discover Serena Williams, a tennis legend. Williams' adventure is riddled with boundaries relating to gender, race, and health, but she continuously demonstrates resilience, grit, and dedication. Her ethos, "I sincerely assume a champion is defined now not thru their wins but with the useful resource of how they might get better after they fall", exemplifies her resilience and highlights the essence of highbrow sturdiness in overcoming setbacks.

Stephen Hawking: Defying Physical Limitations With Mental Might

Stephen Hawking's lifestyles offers a compelling have a observe of mental sturdiness. Diagnosed with a rare shape of motor neuron disease at an early age, he did not permit bodily obstacles to limit his intellectual prowess. His mantra, "However difficult lifestyles may additionally moreover appear, there is usually a few factor you could do and achieve success at," encapsulates his tenacious spirit and resolution to make a contribution to technology, no matter the chances.

Maya Angelou: Rising Above Challenges With the Power of Words

The international of literature offers us Maya Angelou's inspiring existence tale. Despite her tough upbringing marked through using way of racial discrimination and personal trauma, Angelou confirmed highbrow longevity by way of manner of remodeling her past right into a supply of concept. Her terms, "You won't control all of the sports activities that show up to you, but you can determine not to be reduced through them," echo her resilient spirit, underlining her strength of will to upward thrust above her situations.

Nelson Mandela: Unyielding Resolve inside the Face of Injustice

Nelson Mandela, the previous South African President and a key parent in the battle towards apartheid, is a top instance of intellectual sturdiness. Despite 27 years in jail, Mandela remained resolute, gambling a pivotal role in dismantling apartheid. His belief, "The greatest glory in residing lies no longer in in no manner falling, however in developing each time we fall," emphasizes his resilient spirit and belief in staying power.

Oprah Winfrey: From Rags to Riches, a Journey of Resilience

Next, we take a look at Oprah Winfrey, a name synonymous with achievement. From experiencing an impoverished childhood to turning into one of the international's maximum influential girls, Winfrey's journey highlights her resilience and resolution. Her philosophy, "The biggest adventure you can take is to stay the existence of your desires," embodies the essence of mental longevity— embracing disturbing situations and persisting until you advantage your desires.

Elon Musk: Embodying Innovation and Risk-Taking

Finally, we examine Elon Musk, founding father of numerous innovative businesses like Tesla Motors and SpaceX. Known for his audacious visions, Musk's journey is punctuated via way of each screw ups and grand successes. Musk's ethos, "When some thing is critical enough, you do it regardless of the reality that the probabilities aren't for your want," displays his unwavering dedication to his desires, demonstrating resilience in adversity.

These diverse narratives, each serving as a beacon of intellectual sturdiness, show that overcoming restricting ideals and reaching entire functionality is actually possible, no matter the adversities one faces.

5C. STRATEGIES FOR DEVELOPING MENTAL TOUGHNESS

Developing highbrow sturdiness is corresponding to embarking on a adventure packed with every annoying situations and possibilities for increase. The first impediment often encountered is the priority of failure. This fear can act as a deterrent, discouraging us from taking risks or seeking out traumatic conditions because of the tension related to making mistakes and the functionality terrible repercussions that would observe. A big step to overcoming this worry is to change your belief of failure itself. Instead of seeing failure as an illustration of inadequacy or weak spot, you should reframe it as a catalyst for increase and studying. It is vital to understand that errors provide possibilities to refine your techniques and beautify your strategies. Every misstep brings you one step within the route of achievement, and every failure provides in your reservoir of experience and knowledge.

Chapter 8: Battling Self-Doubt

When you encompass failure as an quintessential part of the journey closer to highbrow durability, you open your self to valuable commands and insights which you could not have won in any other case. As people, we frequently grapple with self-doubt, that would considerably impede our improvement in the direction of intellectual toughness. This loss of self-belief and self notion to your abilties can reason procrastination, demotivation, and even self-sabotage. To conquer self-doubt, it will become critical to foster a sense of self confidence and self assurance. This can be completed with the aid of way of regularly education self-affirmation, looking for high quality feedback, putting viable goals, and actively tough terrible self-talk with awesome reinforcement.

Managing Setbacks and Difficulties

Acknowledging your feelings, education self-compassion, and externalizing the manner you revel in are also vital steps on this technique. This proactive technique aids in dismantling self-doubt and lays a strong basis for the development of intellectual durability. It is crucial to understand that the adventure in the direction of intellectual sturdiness is not a right now line. It is full of united states of the united states of americaand downs, moments of progress, and intervals of setbacks. These times have to now not be seen as signs of failure however as an alternative as possibilities to workout and bolster your mental sturdiness. They offer possibilities to use the strategies and device discovered and to navigate via hardships with resilience and grit.

Maintaining Emotional Balance

Through moments of adversity, we can broaden and decorate intellectual fortitude. Building highbrow sturdiness isn't approximately suppressing emotions or adopting a stoic facade. Rather, it's miles approximately fostering resilience and versatility and maintaining a excessive outstanding mind-set amidst adversity. Mental sturdiness includes cultivating emotional stability, because of this recognizing, acknowledging, and dealing with your feelings correctly. Connecting with others who help your adventure, maintaining a hopeful outlook, and looking after yourself physically and emotionally are essential to this method.

Embracing Change

Another common roadblock in the adventure towards intellectual durability is resistance to change. We people are regular creatures, and the idea of changing prolonged-reputation behavior may be intimidating. However, growing mental longevity necessitates confronting the ones fears and embracing uncertainty. Overcoming resistance includes expertise the supply of your fears, reframing trade as an possibility in choice to a danger, visualizing the preferred final results, and taking small, ability steps towards trade. By doing so, you may progressively overcome resistance and make the manner of cultivating intellectual durability greater to be had and lots much less daunting.

Cultivating a Growth Mindset

Nurturing a boom mind-set is crucial for highbrow durability— it allows you bear in mind that abilities can be advanced through strength of will and hard paintings. With a increase mind-set, feelings of helplessness that regularly accompany boundaries may be correctly combated, because of this fostering resilience and improving intellectual sturdiness. This mind-set additionally encourages you to hold topics in thoughts-set and persist in the face of adversity.

The Continuous Journey of Mental Toughness

Developing intellectual durability isn't a one-time occasion. It is ready relentlessly pursuing growth and development and viewing every undertaking as an opportunity. Remember, on this journey, you are not by myself. This e-book, your allies, and your internal fortitude are your guides, supporting you every step of the manner on your route inside the course of highbrow durability.

5D: 10 EXERCISES TO BUILD MENTAL TOUGHNESS

Strengthening highbrow longevity and resilience is an ongoing way that can be fostered thru each day workout. Building the ones talents can frequently start with demanding situations that push you out of your comfort region.

Exercise 1: Take bloodless showers. While to start with uncomfortable, this workout will now not only invigorate your senses however additionally let you include ache and workout manage over your reactions. Over time, this can beautify your functionality to cope with strain and adversity, contributing to mental durability.

Exercise 2: Wait a couple of minutes earlier than you consume while you are hungry.

While it sounds simple, this hobby is a test of staying electricity and electricity of thoughts. It encourages you to differentiate among your need and goals, fostering a enjoy of area and self-restraint.

Exercise three: Do what you least want to do. Dedicating even a hint time, say ten mins, to a challenge you have got been heading off or dreading, will let you face your fears or reluctance. This now not most effective facilitates overcome procrastination but additionally strengthens your resilience to confront tough duties.

Exercise four: Work out with out distractions like music or tv may be an effective exercising. This exercise requires a high degree of attention and willpower. It affords an possibility to concentrate to your thoughts and feelings, fostering mindfulness and highbrow endurance.

Exercise five: Acknowledge and sit down down down together with your emotions, irrespective of whether or not they cause pain. This exercise permits you grow to be more aware of your emotional states and complements your ability to control and alter emotions successfully.

Exercise 6: Identify and label your emotions. This can pass hand in hand with the method above. After you are taking a seat collectively together with your emotions, label them like they will be a technological understanding undertaking. This workout allow you to benefit clarity and manage over your emotional responses, allowing you to navigate tough conditions with extra resilience. When you may name your feelings, you'll higher apprehend what they're, why you enjoy them, and the manner you may manner them while staying emotionally healthful.

Exercise 7: Focus in your breath. Deep respiratory bodily games play a large characteristic in developing intellectual durability. By focusing for your breath, you can not first-class lessen strain and anxiety however moreover increase your focus and recognition. Deep respiratory gives a enjoy of calm and clarity that lets in with choice-making and emotional law.

Exercise eight: Voice your emotions. Having sincere conversations with others is a few other beneficial exercise. Talking approximately your feelings, fears, and aspirations with someone you take delivery of as true with can provide emotional consolation and a sparkling thoughts-set. It will assist you articulate your mind, recognize your feelings higher, and collect help and encouragement.

Exercise 9: Appreciate what you have had been given. Practicing gratitude is likewise an effective way to bring together highbrow sturdiness. By appreciating what you have got were given, you domesticate a exquisite attitude. This outlook permit you to navigate life's challenges with greater grace and resilience.

Exercise 10: Admit your mistakes. This is a critical step toward constructing highbrow durability. Accepting your faults in preference to ignoring or denying them helps you look at and broaden. It additionally fosters humility, a boom thoughts-set, and the braveness to take duty in your moves.

Incorporating those every day sporting events into your routine can substantially beautify intellectual durability and resilience over the years. Each of those practices will push you to step from your consolation place, face your fears, and encompass increase, thereby fostering intellectual durability and resilience.

5E. INTERACTIVE ELEMENT

Mental sturdiness, a fusion of resilience and nicely-being, may be fostered thru interventions grounded in fine psychology. Let's discover an entire lot of smooth but effective physical video video games that could come to be a staple on your every day regular.

The Power of Mindfulness Meditation

A well-known exercise with showed strain-lowering benefits is mindfulness meditation. By cultivating an cognizance of the present, this exercise permits you to discover your thoughts and emotions with out judgment. Consider this a device for mitigating terrible feelings and disempowering beliefs. An handy instance is a 5-minute meditation focusing on your breath. Maintain cognizance of your respiration without trying to manage it. If your thoughts wanders, gently deliver your hobby lower returned for your breath. Through ordinary exercising, this workout can beautify your capability to address pressure and adversity.

Embracing Gratitude: The Path to Positive Mindset

Another device for fortifying intellectual sturdiness is gratitude journaling, seemed to beautify happiness and even beautify physical fitness. Spend a few moments every day writing down three property you are grateful for. These can be clean joys like a comforting cup of espresso or a trap-up call with a pal. This workout can redirect your interest from shortage to abundance, fostering a greater fit thoughts-set.

We frequently forget to renowned our personal strengths and achievements. Recognizing those can make stronger self-esteem, boom self belief, pave the manner to resilience, and ultimately, empower you to confront challenges without faltering.

Grounded in excellent psychology, the activity of reclaiming your strengths consists of energetic reflected picture to your competencies and past successes. Positive psychology asserts that focusing on your strengths rather than your weaknesses and appreciating what is right with you in preference to what is inaccurate can bring about stepped forward happiness and fulfillment.

Strength Identification

To begin, devote some quiet time to listing your non-public strengths. These strengths can be various inclinations, skills, or skills you possess. Are you empathetic and able to recognize and share the emotions of others? Are you inventive and able to overcoming issues in smart strategies? Or likely you are an great listener or an first-rate communicator. Whatever those strengths might be, spotting them can assist enhance a exceptional self-photo.

6UPGRADE YOURSELF

you ever perplexed in case you're sincerely able to changing who you are? Do you enjoy trapped via the person traits you've got been born with, or do you keep in mind that you have the power to convert your self into the individual you need to be? The choose out of this financial disaster may also prompt you to ascertain a excessive-tech technological know-how fiction scenario in which people merge with machines for a superhuman destiny. But in reality, "upgrading yourself" is an normal, human organisation. It includes reshaping your mind, broadening your attitude, and refining your capabilities to comply right into a better model of yourself. Each day gives an possibility to examine, increase, and improve to grow to be more resilient, extra fulfilled, and better prepared to navigate the united statesand downs of lifestyles.

Life isn't always a right away path with a predetermined endpoint however a non-stop adventure of discovery and transformation. And you aren't actually a passenger in this journey but the driving force. You have the power to steer the course you take in your journey; upgrade your mindset, abilities, and behaviors; and craft a existence that aligns collectively alongside your values, passions, and cause.

Consider this: Our smart phones and devices require normal updates and improvements to function optimally. They want to comply to the modern-day-day day software program, fix any bugs, and enhance their fashionable performance. As humans, we can also gain from regular enhancements. To usually check and adapt, refine our competencies, make bigger our expertise, and enhance our mind-set so we will hold up with the ever-changing panorama of existence.

You don't have to try for perfection or take a look at yourself to others. Instead, recognize your functionality for increase and take steps, however small, toward turning into the individual you aspire to be. Learn out of your research, embody your strengths and weaknesses, and remodel disturbing situations into opportunities for growth. When you domesticate a growth mind-set, you view disturbing conditions as possibilities to look at and extend.

Chapter 9: Understanding the Power of Beliefs

In this financial disaster, we dive deep into the captivating international of beliefs and discover their profound effect on our lives. Beliefs are the lenses via which we apprehend the vicinity, shaping our thoughts, emotions, and behaviors. By know-how the electricity of beliefs, we are capable of gain extra manipulate over our lives and free up our whole functionality.

We begin via examining the origins of ideals and the way they may be fashioned. Beliefs can be inspired with the resource of the use of different factors, which encompass our upbringing, way of existence, schooling, and personal studies. We find out the concept of cognitive biases and the manner they might shape our ideals, once in a while essential to distorted wondering styles.

Next, we delve into the particular styles of beliefs that exist. From center ideals that shape our normal worldview, to particular ideals about ourselves, others, and the world round us. We speak the area of each empowering and restricting ideals and the way they will be successful to influence our vanity, self warranty, and choice-making.

To assist readers advantage a deeper expertise in their personal beliefs, we provide practical sports and reflection questions for the duration of the bankruptcy. These sports activities encourage self-mirrored image and introspection, allowing people to find out their center ideals and feature a look at whether or now not or not they are serving them or protective they returned.

Furthermore, we find out the concept of perception systems and the way they will be able to create a framework for our mind, feelings, and moves. We speak the electricity of high great affirmations and visualization strategies in reshaping our beliefs and developing a greater extremely good mind-set.

The monetary smash moreover delves into the idea of perception change and the manner human beings can venture and modify their cutting-edge-day beliefs. We communicate proof-primarily based strategies together with cognitive restructuring, reframing, and exposure remedy, that could help humans overcome proscribing ideals and growth more empowering ones.

Identifying Your Limiting Beliefs

In this financial ruin, we will delve into the manner of identifying and know-how your restricting ideals. Limiting ideals are deeply ingrained mind or beliefs that hold you lower back from accomplishing your whole functionality. They can stem from past reviews, societal conditioning, or self-doubt.

To start, it's far vital to increase self-reputation and recognize the presence of limiting beliefs for your existence. This can be finished thru introspection and reflection. Take a while to do not forget areas for your life in that you feel stuck or wherein you continuously face worrying situations. These areas may also moreover provide clues to the limiting beliefs which may be retaining you again.

Once you've got diagnosed the ones areas, it is important to undertaking and question your beliefs. Ask your self why you preserve those ideals and if they're serving you in a remarkable manner. Often, we adopt proscribing beliefs without virtually examining their validity or thinking about alternative perspectives.

To assist you on this method, you may strive journaling or speakme to a trusted friend or therapist. Writing down your thoughts and emotions can offer readability and permit you to advantage new insights into your ideals. Discussing your ideals with others can offer one-of-a-type perspectives and help you challenge and reframe them.

Additionally, it is able to be beneficial to discover the origins of your proscribing beliefs. Understanding in which they arrive from can offer precious context and help in developing techniques to triumph over them. This also can contain revisiting beyond reports, adolescence upbringing, or cultural impacts.

Challenging and Rewriting Your Beliefs

In this financial disaster, we're able to delve into the system of tough and rewriting your beliefs to foster private increase and triumph over boundaries. Our ideals play a extensive function in shaping our thoughts, feelings, and moves. Sometimes, those ideals may be limiting and hold us back from reaching our complete potential. By getting to know to check and assignment those beliefs, we are able to reshape them in a way that empowers us and lets in us thrive.

To begin with, it's miles important to emerge as aware of the beliefs which is probably currently influencing your lifestyles. This may be finished through introspection and self-reflection. Pay hobby to the thoughts and self-talk that arise in one among a type situations. Notice any everyday styles or bad self-perceptions that may be rooted in underlying beliefs.

Once you have got got diagnosed those ideals, the subsequent step is to assess their validity and accuracy. Ask yourself whether or not there can be concrete evidence to assist those ideals or if they're primarily based totally on assumptions or past reviews that can't be relevant. It's crucial to method this approach with an open mind and a willingness to mission lengthy-held beliefs.

Next, it's time to rewrite the ones ideals in a manner that serves your increase and properly-being. Start with the aid of reframing terrible or restricting beliefs into extra extremely good and empowering statements. For instance, when you have a notion that you aren't precise enough, reframe it as "I am succesful and deserving of achievement." By consciously deciding on new, empowering beliefs, you can rewire your mind to expect in more remarkable and optimistic tactics.

It's critical to enhance those new ideals through consistent exercising and repetition. Affirmations and visualization techniques may be helpful in this method. Write down your new ideals and repeat them regularly, visualizing yourself residing normal with the ones ideals. Over time, these new ideals turns into ingrained on your subconscious thoughts, number one to a shift for your thoughts, feelings, and behaviors.

Furthermore, searching out resource from others may be beneficial at some point of this approach. Sharing your adventure with depended on friends, own family people, or a therapist can provide precious insights and encouragement. They can offer unique views and help you assignment any lingering doubts or resistance.

Remember, tough and rewriting your ideals is an ongoing way. As you continue to expand and evolve, new ideals may additionally come to the surface that requires examination and transformation. Embrace this journey of self-discovery and self-improvement, and be open to the possibilities that lie in advance.

Chapter 10: Overcoming Self-Doubt

In this bankruptcy, we are able to discover diverse strategies and techniques to assist human beings conquer self-doubt. Self-doubt may be a vast barrier to private increase and success; however with the right attitude and tools, it is feasible to conquer it.

Understanding the roots of self-doubt: We will delve into the underlying motives of self-doubt, along facet beyond studies, bad self-communicate, and external affects. By gaining belief into the ones elements, people can better apprehend why they doubt themselves and start to task the ones beliefs.

Cultivating self-recognition: Self-recognition is a important detail of overcoming self-doubt. Through introspection and reflection, humans can turn out to be aware of their strengths, weaknesses, and triggers that contribute to self-doubt. This self-reputation permits for targeted interventions to deal with precise areas of mission.

Challenging terrible self-speak: Negative self-communicate is a commonplace manifestation of self-doubt. We will discover strategies together with cognitive restructuring and best affirmations to counteract terrible thoughts and replace them with empowering and supportive ones.

Setting realistic dreams: Unrealistic expectancies regularly fuel self-doubt. By placing practical and plausible desires, humans can build self warranty and show to themselves that they're capable of achievement. We will talk techniques for putting SMART (Specific, Measurable, Achievable, Relevant, Time-certain) dreams and breaking them down into smaller, capability steps.

Building a manual network: Surrounding oneself with excessive nice and supportive human beings can offer a valuable decorate in overcoming self-doubt. We will discover the significance of looking for mentors, friends, or assist agencies who can provide steering, encouragement, and obligation.

Celebrating successes: Recognizing and celebrating non-public achievements, regardless of how small, is critical in stopping self-doubt. We will communicate the significance of acknowledging improvement, embracing failures as studying possibilities, and working toward self-compassion throughout the adventure.

Cultivating a Growth Mindset

In this bankruptcy, we delve into the concept of a increase thoughts-set and find out techniques to growth and cultivate it. A increase thoughts-set is the notion that one's capabilities and intelligence may be superior via strength of will, try, and resilience. It is a effective thoughts-set that may bring about private and expert boom, increased motivation, and superior problem-solving capabilities.

To start, we speak the importance of self-mirrored image and self-focus in cultivating a boom thoughts-set. By examining our very very own mind and beliefs, we can understand fixed thoughts-set dispositions and work in the direction of replacing them with a increase mind-set. This includes tough terrible self-communicate, reframing failures as learning possibilities, and embracing disturbing conditions as a way for boom.

We then circulate directly to explore the strength of try and perseverance in developing a boom mindset. Through planned exercise and constant effort, people can enhance their capabilities and talents. We provide practical techniques for putting goals, breaking them down into doable steps, and maintaining motivation within the direction of the journey.

Additionally, we communicate the feature of feedback and the way it can be used to foster a growth mind-set. By trying to find comments from others, we benefit precious insights that would help us turn out to be aware of regions for improvement and guide our studying method. We moreover emphasize the importance of supplying super comments to others, as it can make contributions to their increase and development as well.

Another important element of cultivating a growth attitude is embracing annoying conditions and viewing them as opportunities for growth. We discover techniques for stepping out of consolation zones, taking dangers, and developing resilience within the face of setbacks. By reframing traumatic situations as exciting opportunities, humans can overcome limitations and hold to investigate and growth.

Lastly, we speak the significance of cultivating a super and supportive gaining knowledge of environment. We find out strategies to foster collaboration, inspire a boom mind-set in others, and have a great time successes. By surrounding ourselves with like-minded those who share a boom attitude, we are capable of create a supportive community that fosters non-forestall studying and growth.

Harnessing the Power of Positive Affirmations

In this financial disaster, we are able to discover the transformative effects of first-rate affirmations and the manner they're capable of assist humans overcome self-doubt, enhance conceitedness, and obtain their dreams. Positive affirmations are powerful gadget that permit human beings to reprogram their subconscious thoughts and replace lousy thoughts and ideals with exquisite ones.

The financial ruin will begin via the use of explaining the idea of first-rate affirmations and their significance in shaping our mind-set and commonplace nicely-being. It will delve into the technological expertise in the again of affirmations, discussing how they may rewire neural pathways inside the brain and create new, empowering beliefs.

Next, the financial destroy will offer sensible steerage on the way to create and use exquisite affirmations correctly. It will provide step-with the resource of-step instructions on crafting affirmations that resonate with personal goals and aspirations. Additionally, it is going to talk techniques to triumph over resistance to affirmations and maximize their impact.

The monetary catastrophe will then explore considered one in every of a type strategies for incorporating superb affirmations into each day lifestyles. It will communicate the significance of repetition and consistency in reinforcing powerful beliefs, and offer guidelines on integrating affirmations into morning and middle of the night sporting activities, in addition to at a few stage in the day.

Furthermore, the financial disaster will highlight the significance of self-compassion and self-forgiveness in the affirmations way. It will emphasize the want to cope with oneself with kindness and facts, and offer guidance on the usage of affirmations to domesticate self-love and recognition.

Lastly, the chapter wills characteristic inspiring fulfillment reminiscences of humans who have used excessive exceptional affirmations to conquer disturbing situations and obtain their dreams. These actual-life examples will serve as motivation and encouragement for readers to harness the energy of affirmations of their very very personal lives.

Building Self-Confidence

In this financial disaster, we are able to discover unique techniques and strategies to help individuals assemble self-self notion. Self-self warranty performs a crucial feature in our private and expert lives, because it allows us to remember in ourselves and our capabilities. Whether you're searching for to boom your self-self assurance for a way interview, a social occasion, or really in fashionable, this monetary wreck will offer you with realistic guidelines to help you for your journey.

Firstly, it is essential to apprehend that constructing self-self perception is a manner that takes effort and time. It isn't a few issue that may be accomplished in a single day, however with everyday exercise and determination, you could step by step boom your self notion ranges. One effective approach is to set sensible desires for your self. By setting capability dreams and working inside the direction of them, you could enjoy small victories along the way, as a manner to enhance your self belief.

Another technique to build self-confidence is to assignment awful self-communicate. Often, our very very very own inner voice can be our most harsh critic, continuously undermining our shallowness. By identifying horrible thoughts and converting them with extremely good and empowering ones, you can begin to change your attitude and construct a more high satisfactory self-photo.

Additionally, surrounding yourself with incredible and supportive people can considerably effect yourself-self assure. Negative impacts can carry you down and make it tougher to accept as true with in yourself. On the possibility hand, being around folks who consider in you and resource you can provide a useful supply of encouragement and motivation.

Furthermore, searching after your bodily and intellectual well-being also can make contributions to building self-self assure. Engaging in everyday workout, eating a balanced weight loss plan, and getting sufficient sleep can help improve your trendy enjoy of self confidence. Additionally, strolling within the course of self-care sports activities which consist of meditation, journaling, or carrying out pursuits that supply you satisfaction can also enhance yourself notion.

Finally, it's miles important to have an superb time your achievements, no matter how small they may seem. Acknowledging and celebrating your successes will beautify top notch behaviors and assist you assemble a robust basis of self-self assurance.

Developing Resilience within the Face of Challenges

Resilience is the capability to get higher from adversity and keep a pleasant attitude in the face of stressful conditions. In this bankruptcy, we are able to discover various techniques and strategies which could help human beings increase resilience and conquer limitations.

Understanding Resilience:

Definition of resilience and its importance in personal growth and development.

Exploring the idea of "get higher" and the way it pertains to resilience.

Examining the distinction among resilience and resistance.

Identifying Personal Strengths:

Assessing personal strengths and spotting regions of resilience.

Understanding the location of self-focus in developing resilience.

Identifying and leveraging non-public sources and manual systems.

Building Emotional Resilience:

Cultivating emotional intelligence and self-law skills.

Developing powerful coping mechanisms for managing pressure and adversity.

Exploring the power of first-rate wondering and reframing poor research.

Developing Cognitive Resilience:

Enhancing problem-fixing capabilities and adaptive wondering.

Overcoming cognitive biases and cultivating a increase thoughts-set.

Strengthening cognitive flexibility and flexibility.

Nurturing Physical Resilience:

Understanding the thoughts-frame connection and the effect of bodily fitness on resilience.

Establishing wholesome way of life behavior, at the side of exercise, nutrients, and sleep.

Exploring relaxation strategies and the characteristic of mindfulness in physical resilience.

Cultivating Social Resilience:

Building robust social connections and manual networks.

Developing powerful communique and warfare selection skills.

Understanding the importance of empathy and compassion in resilience.

Embracing Change and Uncertainty:

Developing flexibility and adaptability in the face of exchange.

Learning to encompass uncertainty and recall it as an opportunity for boom.

Exploring techniques for dealing with worry and tension related to trade.

Overcoming Setbacks and Failure:

Understanding the area of failure in resilience and private boom.

Developing a healthy dating with failure and gaining knowledge of from setbacks.

Cultivating perseverance and resilience within the face of adversity.

Chapter 11: Creating A Supportive Environment

In this bankruptcy, we are able to talk the significance of making supportive surroundings for folks who are going through fears, tension, stress, or a few other shape of mental or emotional annoying conditions. A supportive environment plays a important function in assisting people sense secure, understood, and endorsed to triumph over their problems.

Setting the Tone: The first step in developing a supportive environment is putting the proper tone. This includes growing a non-judgmental and empathetic atmosphere wherein people feel snug expressing their thoughts and emotions without worry of grievance or rejection. This can be completed through way of fostering open conversation, active listening, and promoting a subculture of appreciate and recognition.

Establishing Boundaries: While creating a supportive environment, it's miles crucial to installation clear obstacles to make sure a secure and healthful area for each person concerned. Boundaries help hold a experience of shape and protect people from any capability damage. It is vital to talk and put into effect the ones barriers normally to create a feel of protection and don't forget.

Providing Emotional Support: A supportive environment must provide emotional help to people who are handling annoying situations. This can embody imparting a listening ear, offering terms of encouragement, and validating their emotions. Additionally, connecting human beings with assist corporations, therapists, or counselors can extensively beautify their emotional well-being.

Encouraging Self-Care: Self-care is an important a part of growing a supportive surroundings. Empowering people to prioritize their nicely-being with the useful resource of challenge sports that sell self-care, collectively with exercising, mindfulness, hobbies, and rest strategies, can assist them construct resilience and deal with their fears and anxieties more efficaciously.

Promoting Collaboration: Collaboration amongst humans in a supportive environment can foster a enjoy of network, shared research, and mutual help. Encouraging company sports activities, peer resource, and collaborative trouble-fixing can create a strong help network that lets in human beings enjoy a whole lot much less isolated and further empowered to stand their demanding situations.

Providing Resources: A supportive surroundings must also provide people with get admission to to assets that may help them of their journey of overcoming fears, tension, and stress. This can include books, articles, on-line courses, workshops, or treatment options that cater to their unique needs.

Celebrating Progress: Celebrating and acknowledging humans' development, irrespective of how small, is a crucial issue of creating a supportive surroundings. Recognizing their efforts and achievements can enhance their self warranty, motivation, and simple properly-being.

Letting Go of Past Failures and Regrets

In this financial disaster, we're capable of discover powerful strategies to help you let go of past disasters and regrets, permitting you to move in advance and live a greater exciting existence. It is herbal for humans to stay on beyond mistakes and sense regret or guilt. However, retaining onto those horrible emotions can save you non-public boom and ward off your capability to prevail inside the future.

To start, it's miles crucial to renowned and receive your past disasters and regrets. Reflect on what befell, why it befell, and the way it has affected you. Take obligation for your actions, but furthermore apprehend that everybody makes mistakes. Remind yourself that the ones evaluations have unique you into the person you are in recent times, presenting precious education and opportunities for growth.

Once you have got were given identified and famous your past disasters and regrets, it is time to permit flow. One powerful technique is to workout self-compassion. Treat yourself with kindness and knowledge, without a doubt as you will a close to buddy. Remind yourself that it's miles good enough to make mistakes and that you deserve forgiveness.

Another useful approach is to reframe your mind-set. Instead of viewing past screw ups as eternal and defining, see them as brief setbacks and opportunities for reading. Focus on the instructions you've got were given obtained and the growth you have got were given skilled. By reframing your thoughts-set, you can shift your consciousness from regret to private improvement.

Additionally, schooling mindfulness can resource in letting skip of beyond disasters and regrets. Mindfulness includes being present in the moment and non-judgmentally looking at your thoughts and emotions. By running closer to mindfulness, you can detach yourself from horrible mind and emotions associated with past screw ups, permitting them to bypass with out clinging onto them.

Finally, it is able to be beneficial to are looking for help from others. Share your testimonies with depended on buddies, family participants, or a therapist. Talking about your regrets and screw ups can provide you with a sparkling thoughts-set and assist you gain closure. Surround your self with wonderful and supportive folks that can encourage and uplift you to your adventure of letting move and transferring in advance.

Embracing Change and Uncertainty

In this economic disaster, we are capable of delve into the problem of embracing trade and uncertainty. Change is an inevitable part of lifestyles, and it could frequently be a deliver of stress and anxiety. However, thru learning to embody alternate and navigate uncertainty, we're able to foster private boom and resilience.

Understanding the individual of change:

Change is a everyday in lifestyles, and resisting it simplest results in frustration and stagnation.

By accepting that alternate is a natural part of the human enjoy, we will method it with a more excessive terrific mind-set.

Cultivating adaptability:

Adaptability is the functionality to regulate to new occasions and worrying conditions.

Through conscious effort and practice, we are able to cultivate adaptability and end up extra snug with exchange.

This involves developing flexible wondering styles and being open to new opportunities.

Overcoming fear of the unknown:

Uncertainty regularly triggers worry and anxiety, as we're wired to are in search of for stability and predictability.

By acknowledging and tough our fears, we're capable of often grow to be more snug with uncertainty.

Techniques together with mindfulness and cognitive reframing can assist us reframe our notion of uncertainty.

Building resilience:

Resilience is the capacity to get better from adversity and navigate thru tough times.

Embracing change and uncertainty can contribute to the improvement of resilience.

By recognizing that setbacks and boundaries are opportunities for growth, we're able to assemble resilience and thrive inside the face of alternate.

Practicing self-care:

Change and uncertainty can be emotionally draining, so it's important to prioritize self-care.

Engaging in sports activities that promote rest, including exercising, meditation, or spending time in nature, can assist alleviate strain and tension.

Taking care of our bodily and highbrow nicely-being allows us to navigate trade greater correctly.

Setting and Achieving Goals

In this economic catastrophe, we're able to find out the significance of setting dreams and a way to correctly gain them. Setting dreams is crucial for personal and professional boom because it offers direction, motivation, and a experience of reason.

Understanding the importance of intention putting:

Goals offer us a easy imaginative and prescient of what we want to gain and assist us stay centered.

They offer a roadmap for achievement and help us measure progress along the manner.

Goal setting complements self-self warranty and vanity even as we accomplish what we got right down to do.

Identifying and prioritizing dreams:

Start with the beneficial useful resource of identifying what you want to acquire, every inside the short time period and long term.

Prioritize your dreams based mostly on their importance and feasibility.

Break down big goals into smaller, doable obligations to steer them to more viable.

Setting SMART goals:

Specific: Define your goals in smooth and precise terms.

Measurable: Ensure that your goals may be measured, so you can tune development.

Achievable: Set dreams that are hard however doable with strive and dedication.

Relevant: Align your desires collectively together with your values and aspirations.

Time-certain: Set ultimate dates in your desires to create a experience of urgency.

Creating an movement plan:

Outline the stairs required to accumulate every purpose.

Break down the responsibilities into smaller, actionable steps.

Assign closing dates to each challenge to stay heading in the proper path.

Regularly assessment and alter your movement plan as wanted.

Overcoming obstacles and staying stimulated:

Anticipate capacity obstacles and develop techniques to conquer them.

Stay added on thru celebrating small victories along the way.

Seek assist from buddies, own family, or mentors to stay accountable and stimulated.

Tracking improvement and making changes:

Regularly evaluate your improvement and make modifications in your dreams and movement plan.

Celebrate milestones and renowned areas for development.

Be bendy and willing to comply your goals as conditions trade.

Chapter 12: Cultivating Self-Compassion

In this financial disaster, we delve into the concept of self-compassion and find out numerous techniques and strategies to cultivate it. Self-compassion refers to the ability to cope with oneself with kindness, information, and recognition, in particular at some point of times of problem, failure, or suffering.

Understanding Self-Compassion:

We start with the useful resource of defining self-compassion and discussing its importance in promoting intellectual nicely-being and emotional resilience.

We discover the three middle components of self-compassion: self-kindness, common humanity, and mindfulness.

Through real-lifestyles examples and study's findings, we illustrate how self-compassion can virtually impact numerous regions of life, together with relationships, artwork, and personal boom.

Practicing Self-Kindness:

We offer practical strategies to domesticate self-kindness, which include self-care practices, great self-talk, and self-soothing sports.

We explore the electricity of self-compassionate language and the way reframing negative self-speak can decorate self-compassion and vanity.

Through guided physical video games and reflections, readers discover ways to make bigger a kinder and further nurturing relationship with themselves.

Embracing Common Humanity:

We speak the idea of common humanity, which emphasizes that suffering and imperfection are traditional studies.

We explore the bad results of self-isolation and the advantages of connecting with others who percentage comparable struggles.

Through storytelling and empathy-constructing bodily games, readers discover ways to cultivate a enjoy of commonplace humanity and expand compassion for themselves and others.

Cultivating Mindfulness:

We introduce mindfulness as a effective device for cultivating self-compassion.

We find out severa mindfulness practices, inclusive of meditation, breath attention, and body test physical sports, which help human beings develop a non-judgmental and accepting mind-set in the path of themselves.

Through step-via-step commands and personal anecdotes, readers are guided on a way to combine mindfulness into their every day lives and use it as a foundation for self-compassion.

Overcoming Obstacles:

We cope with commonplace barriers and disturbing situations that may upward thrust up when cultivating self-compassion.

We provide techniques to triumph over self-grievance, perfectionism, and resistance to self-compassion.

Through carrying events and self-reflected photograph activates, readers discover ways to navigate the ones barriers and boom a resilient and compassionate attitude.

Building Healthy Relationships

In this economic catastrophe, we will discover the importance of building healthy relationships and provide practical techniques for fostering fantastic connections with others. Building and retaining healthful relationships is vital for common nicely-being and may extensively make a contribution to someone's happiness and success.

Understanding the importance of wholesome relationships:

We will start by using the usage of the usage of discussing why healthy relationships are essential. Healthy relationships offer help, companionship, and emotional stability. They can help lessen stress, enhance arrogance, and decorate stylish intellectual and bodily health.

Communication talents:

Effective conversation is the inspiration of a wholesome relationship. We will delve into diverse verbal exchange strategies consisting of lively listening, assertiveness, and non-verbal verbal exchange. These abilities are important for expressing one's thoughts, emotions, and wishes at the equal time as moreover expertise and empathizing with others.

Building accept as proper with and respect:

Trust and recognize are crucial components of healthful relationships. We will discover approaches to construct recollect, collectively with being dependable, keeping guarantees, and retaining confidentiality. Additionally, we are in a role to speak about the importance of respecting boundaries, evaluations, and variations in a courting.

Conflict decision:

Conflict is inevitable in any courting. However, how we cope with conflicts should make a large difference. We will offer strategies for effective struggle selection, which include lively listening, empathy, compromise, and locating win-win answers. Understanding and dealing with emotions in the route of conflicts also can be discussed.

Nurturing emotional intimacy:

Emotional intimacy is the deep emotional connection among people. We will find out techniques to nurture emotional intimacy, in conjunction with expressing vulnerability, displaying empathy, and education emotional help. We might also talk the significance of preserving a healthful stability among independence and interdependence in a dating.

Building resilience in relationships:

Relationships face annoying conditions and setbacks. Building resilience is essential for navigating thru tough instances. We will offer techniques for building resilience, which encompass growing problem-solving abilties, preserving a excellent mind-set, and looking for useful resource from others.

Boundaries and self-care:

Establishing and maintaining healthy barriers is vital for a thriving relationship. We will talk the significance of setting limitations and prioritizing self-care to ensure the properly-being of every humans in a courting. We will explore self-care practices that would assist humans hold their intellectual, emotional, and physical fitness.

Chapter 13: Mindfulness and Creativity

Mindfulness and creativity are two mind that complement each distinct fantastically. Mindfulness, the exercise of being surely gift and conscious inside the 2d, can substantially enhance one's creativity. By cultivating a aware united states of america of thoughts, individuals can tap into their inner creativity and unfastened up their entire potential.

In this bankruptcy, we are capable of explore the relationship amongst mindfulness and creativity and delve into numerous techniques and physical games that could assist individuals harness their cutting-edge skills through mindfulness.

Understanding the modern technique: We will start through inspecting the creative tool and the way mindfulness can play a vital function in every stage. From generating mind to refining them, mindfulness can help human beings live targeted, open-minded, and receptive to new possibilities.

Cultivating a modern thoughts-set: We will communicate how mindfulness can assist individuals adopt a progressive mind-set by way of manner of fostering hobby, embracing uncertainty, and letting flow into of self-judgment. Through mindfulness, human beings can overcome modern blocks and get right of entry to their innate progressive ability.

Mindful declaration: We will find out techniques for mindfully looking the arena round us, on the aspect of conscious taking walks, aware listening, and aware seeing. By appealing our senses and being fully present, we're capable of tap into the richness of our environment, sparking new mind and perspectives.

Mindful creativity wearing activities: This monetary disaster also can even consist of a range of mindfulness-based absolutely absolutely physical sports in particular designed to decorate creativity. These bodily activities also can additionally consist of aware doodling, conscious writing, and conscious storytelling. By bringing mindfulness to our creative endeavors, we can get right of entry to a country of flow and tap into our internal most wells of thought.

Mindfulness and innovative expression: Finally, we're able to explore how mindfulness can beautify severa forms of modern expression, collectively with painting, writing, music, and dance. By cultivating a aware state of being, human beings can infuse their modern paintings with depth, authenticity, and emotional resonance.

Mindfulness and Resilience

In this financial disaster, we're able to find out the powerful connection among mindfulness and resilience. Mindfulness is a workout that includes listening to the present 2d, with out judgment. It has been used for hundreds of years in severa cultures and is now gaining reputation in Western psychology for its numerous advantages.

Resilience, rather, refers to the capacity to get better from adversity and maintain intellectual well-being within the face of stressful conditions. It is a vital expertise to have in present day speedy-paced and unpredictable worldwide.

Mindfulness can significantly beautify resilience with the resource of using allowing individuals to boom a more focus of their thoughts, emotions, and physical sensations. By being gift in the second, humans can gain treasured insights into their very non-public kinds of questioning and reacting, that might then be used to domesticate resilience.

One of the important thing techniques mindfulness promotes resilience is with the resource of the usage of decreasing strain. When we are aware, we're higher able to understand stressors and reply to them in a more calm and composed way. This facilitates prevent the bad effects of continual stress on our bodily and highbrow health.

Additionally, mindfulness helps people domesticate a more sense of self-compassion. By training non-judgmental hobby, human beings can growth a kind and accepting mind-set closer to themselves, even in the face of failure or setbacks. This self-compassion acts as a defensive factor toward the terrible effects of pressure and promotes resilience.

Furthermore, mindfulness can beautify cognitive flexibility, this is an important issue of resilience. By being gift inside the 2d and looking our mind, we are able to end up aware about any rigid or negative wondering styles that could prevent our ability to evolve and bounce back from adversity. Through mindfulness, we can domesticate a greater open and bendy attitude, allowing us to discover innovative answers to problems and navigate challenges extra successfully.

In this bankruptcy, we are able to discover numerous mindfulness practices and techniques that can be used to beautify resilience. We will discover ways to domesticate present-moment cognizance, boom self-compassion, and cultivate cognitive flexibility. We can also discover the characteristic of mindfulness in building social useful resource networks and fostering super relationships, which may be essential for resilience.

Sustaining Your Growth and Transformation

In this financial disaster, we're able to discover ways to keep your increase and transformation after overcoming fears, tension, and stress. Sustaining private boom and transformation is crucial for long-term nicely-being and continued development. Here are some key factors to keep in mind:

Reflecting in your adventure: Take time to mirror on the improvement you've got got made thus far. Recognize and have amusing your achievements, every massive and small. Reflecting on your adventure can help you stay recommended and make stronger your determination to non-public increase.

Setting new dreams: As you maintain on your route of increase and transformation, it's miles critical to set new dreams for your self. These dreams can be associated with non-public improvement, career advancement, relationships, or a few different place of your existence that you wish to enhance. Setting dreams keeps you focused and gives a experience of cause.

Continuing schooling and reading: Never forestall getting to know. Seek out new records and competencies that align together together with your hobbies and aspirations. This may be carried out thru reading books, attending workshops or seminars, taking on line guides, or wearing out huge conversations with specialists to your vicinity of interest.

Surrounding yourself with supportive human beings: Surrounding your self with outstanding and supportive individuals ought to make a sizeable distinction to your adventure of growth and transformation.

Seek out like-minded individuals who encourage and inspire you. Share your desires and aspirations with them, and they could provide treasured guidance and assist.

Practicing self-care: Taking care of yourself is essential for sustaining increase and transformation. Make self-care a priority by means of incorporating sports that convey you joy and relaxation into your each day habitual. This can encompass workout, meditation, spending time in nature, undertaking interests, or in truth taking time to relaxation and rejuvenate.

Embracing demanding conditions: Growth and transformation frequently involve coping with new stressful conditions and stepping out of your consolation area. Embrace the ones demanding situations as possibilities for private growth. Embracing disturbing conditions allows you construct resilience and self guarantee in your capability to overcome barriers.

Staying aware and present: Mindfulness performs a critical function in maintaining boom and transformation. Practice being honestly gift inside the second, watching your mind and feelings without judgment. Mindfulness permits you stay grounded and centered, allowing you to make conscious picks that align alongside side your values and goals.

Celebrating development: Finally, keep in mind to have amusing your development along the manner. Acknowledge and admire how a protracted way you have got come, and supply your self credit score rating for the efforts you've got have been given placed into your private boom and transformation. Celebrating development reinforces extraordinary conduct and motivates you to preserve to your adventure.

Chapter 14: Acknowledging the Mountain Within

Great! Let's start with a definition of the "mountain internal." This mountain is a metaphor for the internal obstacles that stand in our manner, collectively with fear, self-doubt, and limiting beliefs. These barriers may additionally seem insurmountable; however the first step to overcoming them is genuinely acknowledging their lifestyles.

Understanding the boundaries that preserve us decrease lower back

Understanding the limitations that maintain us returned is a important issue of acknowledging the mountain interior. This metaphorical mountain represents the worrying situations, fears, and boundaries that beat back our personal and expert growth. Exploring the ones obstacles permits us to advantage perception into our very personal psyche, paving the manner for self-discovery and transformation.

One large barrier is the priority of failure. This fear regularly stems from societal expectations, perfectionism, or past reports. It creates a intellectual block that forestalls humans from taking risks and pursuing their desires. To extensively recognized the mountain inner, one should confront and recognize this fear, recognizing that failure is not an everlasting setback however a stepping stone toward fulfillment.

Another barrier is self-doubt, which may be fueled through imposter syndrome or a lack of self assurance. Acknowledging the mountain inner entails tough those terrible self-perceptions and information that everybody faces moments of uncertainty. By building self-esteem and embracing a increase attitude, individuals can overcome self-doubt and reach new heights.

Comfort zones moreover act as formidable boundaries at the course to self-discovery. The familiarity of habitual can also provide a sense of security, but it often limits private and professional development. To renowned the mountain internal, one must be inclined to step out of doors the comfort zone, embody exchange, and confront the annoying situations that consist of personal boom.

Moreover, outside expectancies and societal norms can create limitations that ward off proper self-expression. Whether stimulated with the aid of cultural, familial, or societal pressures, human beings can also discover it tough to interrupt loose from expectations that don't align with their real selves. Acknowledging the mountain inside includes recognizing and tough those outside impacts, considering a greater actual and fantastic adventure.

Perceived lack of assets or opportunities is some different barrier that holds many again. It's crucial to apprehend that the mountain inside isn't always insurmountable; as an alternative, it requires resourcefulness and resilience. By reframing challenges as possibilities for revolutionary trouble-fixing, humans can overcome boundaries and tap into their whole potential.

Fear of judgment and criticism additionally can be a great obstacle at the path to self-discovery. Acknowledging the mountain internal includes data that everybody faces scrutiny in some unspecified time inside the destiny and that real increase regularly consists of navigating through the ones outdoor critiques. Developing emotional resilience and a robust sense of self can assist individuals conquer the concern of judgment.

Procrastination and a loss of concern make a contribution to the mountain inside by means of manner of delaying development. Understanding the highbrow motives at the back of procrastination, alongside aspect worry of failure or perfectionism, is essential. Acknowledging the mountain inner calls for growing effective time control talents, putting sensible dreams, and breaking down obligations into feasible steps.

Understanding the regulations that hold us decrease back is an essential part of acknowledging the mountain interior. Fear of failure, self-doubt, comfort zones, outside expectancies, useful aid obstacles, fear of judgment, and procrastination are all formidable limitations that people should confront on their adventure of self-discovery. By addressing those barriers head-on, humans can begin the ascent of their metaphorical mountain, gaining a deeper expertise of themselves and unlocking their full ability.

Overcoming Negative Self Talks

Overcoming Negative Self-Talk. Negative self-talk is a not unusual manner that self-limiting ideals seem. This is on the identical time as you constantly criticize and determine yourself, including telling your self "I'm a failure" or "I'm no longer unique sufficient." This may be a vicious cycle that maintains you stuck in a terrible mindset.

Acknowledging the mountain inside is a metaphorical journey inside the course of self-discovery and private increase. However, as we traverse this path, we frequently stumble upon the formidable assignment of terrible self-talks that might act as insidious roadblocks, impeding our improvement and clouding the summit of our capability. In this exploration, we delve into the techniques and mind-set shifts critical to triumph over those self-imposed limitations and ascend the metaphorical mountain inner.

Negative self-talks are the internal narratives we construct about ourselves, shaping our perceptions, ideals, and movements. These narratives may be deeply ingrained, inspired via manner of beyond studies, societal expectancies, or even unfounded fears. Recognizing and addressing these horrible scripts is essential to overcoming the restrictions they invent on our adventure to self-discovery.

Firstly, consciousness is the cornerstone of alternate. Acknowledging the lifestyles of terrible self-talks is the initial step towards dismantling their energy. Take a conscious stock of your mind and discover sorts of self-restricting ideals. By information the nature of these mind, you benefit belief into the triggers and origins, permitting you to mission them efficaciously.

Once diagnosed, reframe those lousy mind into excessive first-class affirmations. Transform "I can not try this; I typically fail" into "I am capable of overcoming demanding situations, and every setback is an possibility for increase." By consciously converting negativity with positivity, you little by little reshape your thoughts-set, fostering a more empowering internal communicate.

Cultivating self-compassion is further vital. Understand that everyone encounters issues and makes mistakes. Instead of harsh self-criticism, embody a compassionate stance toward your self. Treat yourself with the identical kindness and information you will make bigger to a friend going via comparable challenges. This shift in perspective fosters resilience and diminishes the effect of horrible self-talks.

Building a strong assist machine is some other important trouble of overcoming terrible self-talks. Surround yourself with individuals who uplift and encourage you. Share your struggles with depended on pals or own family members who offer advantageous feedback and manual. Having a reliable community reinforces exquisite ideals approximately your self and counteracts the keeping apart effects of self-doubt.

Mindfulness practices play a pivotal feature in breaking the cycle of awful self-communicate. Engage in sports sports that convey you into the present 2nd, which encompass meditation or deep breathing bodily video games. Mindfulness permits you to have a look at your mind without judgment, developing a space for intentional responses in preference to reacting abruptly to self-restricting narratives.

Challenge the validity of lousy self-talks thru thinking their accuracy. Ask your self if the ones mind are primarily based on evidence or if they may be distorted perceptions. Often, terrible self-talks are rooted in cognitive distortions – irrational and biased concept styles. By significantly comparing the ones distortions, you dismantle their credibility and pave the manner for extra rational and high nice thinking.

Setting realistic desires and celebrating small victories is instrumental in building self perception and countering awful self-talks. Break down large aspirations into attainable steps, and renowned your achievements along the way. Recognizing development, irrespective of how incremental, reinforces a excellent self-photograph and diminishes the have an effect on of self-proscribing ideals.

Visualizing fulfillment is a remarkable tool in overcoming terrible self-talks. Create a top notch intellectual photograph of your self undertaking your goals. Immerse your self in the feelings and sensations associated with this success. Visualization not quality bolsters confidence but additionally retrains the thoughts to cognizance on opportunities as opposed to barriers.

Embracing a growth mind-set is transformative in preventing negative self-talks. Recognize that abilities can be advanced thru determination and try. Embrace worrying conditions as possibilities to investigate and develop, reframing setbacks as precious evaluations. A boom thoughts-set fosters resilience and diminishes the strength of consistent, self-proscribing beliefs.

In give up, acknowledging the mountain interior encompasses no longer only spotting our functionality however additionally confronting and overcoming the horrific self-talks that ward off our ascent. Through self-interest, satisfactory reframing, self-compassion, assist systems, mindfulness, essential questioning, motive-placing, visualization, and adopting a growth mind-set, we're capable of dismantle the limitations created by using the usage of poor self-talks. As we traverse the direction to self-discovery, these techniques empower us to ascend the metaphorical mountain internal and achieve the summit of our real ability.

Cultivating a Growth Mindset

We can find out "Cultivating a Growth Mindset." A increase mind-set is the alternative of a fixed mindset, it clearly is when you accept as genuine along with your abilties and talents are regular and unchangeable. With a growth thoughts-set, you don't forget that your capabilities may be evolved with attempt and endurance.

Acknowledging the mountain internal is the first step on the journey of self-discovery and personal improvement. This metaphorical mountain represents the disturbing conditions and boundaries we're dealing with in our lives, both internal and out of doors. To overcome this mountain, one need to adopt a growth mindset—a powerful attitude that fosters resilience, reading, and non-forestall improvement.

A increase attitude is the perception that competencies and intelligence can be advanced thru dedication and difficult art work. This contrasts with a set mind-set, which assumes that traits are innate and unchangeable. Embracing a increase mindset transforms the manner we method challenges, setbacks, and the pursuit of our dreams as we ascend the metaphorical mountain inside.

The foundation of a increase mindset lies in facts that screw ups and setbacks aren't signs of inherent boundaries however rather opportunities for mastering and increase. This attitude shift is essential as we encounter the steep slopes and rugged terrain on our journey. Instead of viewing limitations as insurmountable limitations, human beings with a boom mind-set see them as stepping stones to development.

One key detail of cultivating a growth mind-set is reframing our notion of try. In a difficult and fast attitude, effort is often regarded as fruitless if fulfillment isn't instantaneous. However, individuals with a increase mind-set recognize that try is the direction to mastery. They understand that the journey up the mountain requires perseverance, resilience, and a dedication to analyzing from every step, irrespective of the final outcomes.

Furthermore, embracing demanding situations turns into a primary tenet of a increase mind-set. Rather than keeping off problems, people with this mind-set actively are seeking for them out, recognizing that each project gives an possibility to stretch their abilities and increase their skills. As we renowned the mountain inner, it turns into essential to approach its ascent with courage and a willingness to confront the unknown.

Learning from grievance is some extraordinary cornerstone of the increase attitude. Instead of viewing feedback as a personal attack, humans with this mind-set see it as treasured records that might gas their development. Constructive complaint turns into a device for refinement, guiding them as they navigate the intricacies of the ascent.

Chapter 15: Identifying Self-Limiting Beliefs

Let's waft directly to the following section, "Identifying Self-Limiting Beliefs." Self-proscribing beliefs are negative mind or assumptions that we've got got have been given about ourselves, which include "I'm not pinnacle sufficient" or "I'll in no way prevail." They can stem from past reviews or social conditioning, and they may prevent us from taking dangers, trying new topics, or attaining our entire functionality.

Recognizing the belief styles that maintain us stuck.

Recognizing the idea styles that preserve us stuck is essential in the journey of identifying and overcoming self-restricting ideals. These patterns frequently characteristic below the ground, influencing our alternatives, actions, and traditional thoughts-set. By bringing them into conscious focus, we empower ourselves to break free from the restrictions imposed via way of those limiting beliefs.

One not unusual concept sample is "catastrophizing," in which human beings habitually expect the worst possible consequences. This pessimistic thoughts-set can prevent private increase, as it fosters worry and tension, stopping us from taking vital risks. Recognizing this pattern includes acknowledging exaggerated thoughts and changing them with a extra balanced mindset.

Another well-known sample is "all-or-no longer whatever wondering," characterised thru viewing situations in excessive, black-and-white terms. This rigid attitude units unrealistic requirements, making it hard to recognize incremental development. Identifying this concept sample calls for cultivating a extra flexible mind-set that acknowledges the sun sunglasses of grey in severa factors of life.

Furthermore, the "imposter syndrome" idea pattern manifests as a persistent worry of being exposed as a fraud irrespective of evidence of competence. This belief can undermine self assure and push back professional advancement. Recognizing imposter syndrome consists of acknowledging achievements and embracing the fact of one's skills.

The "confirmation bias" concept sample leads humans to are looking for for and prioritize records that aligns with their current ideals at the equal time as dismissing opposing views. Recognizing this sample includes actively in search of numerous perspectives and being open to hard one's private assumptions.

Self-sabotage, each other detrimental idea sample, consists of behaviors that undermine private or expert achievement. Identifying self-sabotage calls for introspection to find underlying fears or insecurities that can be using these counterproductive actions.

Furthermore, "constant attitude" wondering inhibits growth via way of assuming that abilities and intelligence are innate and unchangeable. Recognizing this sample consists of embracing a "increase mind-set," acknowledging that talents may be developed thru try to perseverance.

Procrastination is a idea pattern that regularly stems from fear of failure or perfectionism. Recognizing this sample includes understanding the underlying emotions the usage of procrastination and developing strategies to overcome it.

Additionally, the "evaluation entice" idea pattern entails continuously measuring oneself in competition to others, primary to feelings of inadequacy. Recognizing this pattern requires cultivating self-compassion and specializing in private improvement in location of out of doors benchmarks.

Identifying and difficult the ones perception patterns consists of self-focus, mindfulness, and a determination to private development. Journaling, remedy, and nice self-reflected image are valuable tools in this device. By recognizing and dismantling the ones belief styles, humans can pave the manner for a more high-quality and empowering notion gadget that fosters increase, resilience, and success.

Recognizing the idea styles that maintain us stuck is an critical step in identifying and overcoming self-limiting ideals. From catastrophizing and all-or-not anything thinking to imposter syndrome and confirmation bias, know-how these styles empowers people to break unfastened from the limitations that keep away from non-public and professional growth. Through self-popularity and intentional efforts, we are capable of reshape our idea patterns, fostering a mindset that promotes resilience, getting to know, and a fulfilling existence.

Developing Self Efficacy

Self-efficacy, a key aspect of intellectual properly-being, performs a critical function in a unmarried's capability to apprehend and overcome self-restricting ideals. Developing self-efficacy entails cultivating a deep belief in a single's functionality to navigate annoying conditions, have a observe from research, and acquire dreams. In the context of figuring out self-limiting ideals, human beings can beautify their self-efficacy via self-consciousness, cognitive restructuring, and proactive behavioral techniques.

Self-popularity serves as the inspiration for recognizing and hard self-restricting beliefs. By knowledge one's mind, feelings, and behaviors, humans advantage insights into the origins of their proscribing beliefs. This hobby empowers individuals to question the validity of these ideals and discover opportunity perspectives. Regular mirrored image and mindfulness practices can make contributions to heightened self-cognizance, growing a fertile floor for the development of self-efficacy.

Cognitive restructuring is a effective method for remodeling self-limiting beliefs. This approach consists of hard and reframing terrible mind that contribute to emotions of inadequacy or self-doubt. By consciously changing irrational ideals with greater sensible and high-quality ones, individuals can reshape their cognitive panorama. Engaging in cognitive restructuring requires a commitment to self-reflected photograph and a willingness to assignment prolonged-repute ideals that may be preserving one once more.

Moreover, developing self-efficacy includes placing sensible and potential desires. Breaking down big objectives into smaller, viable duties lets in human beings to assemble a sense of competence and accomplishment. Success in those smaller responsibilities contributes to a high-quality feedback loop, reinforcing the notion in one's functionality to overcome worrying situations. Celebrating achievements, irrespective of how small, nurtures a increase mind-set and bolsters self-efficacy.

Chapter 16: Overcoming Self Doubt

Breaking lousy perception styles

Breaking horrible idea styles is a critical step in overcoming self-doubt and fostering a nice mind-set. Self-doubt can be insidious, weaving its manner into our thoughts and influencing our belief of ourselves. However, via spotting and hard horrible idea patterns, we are able to shift our mindset and gather extra self-self assurance.

One commonplace negative idea pattern is "catastrophizing," wherein people envision the worst feasible final outcomes of a situation. To ruin this sample, it's miles vital to pause and objectively verify the state of affairs. Ask yourself in case your thoughts are based totally totally mostly on information or assumptions. Often, the truth is a lot much much less dire than our hectic minds make it out to be.

Another adverse sample is "personalization," in which individuals function terrible events to themselves, even when they may be not immediately accountable. Overcoming this pattern entails acknowledging that now not the whole lot is ready us and recognizing out of doors elements that make contributions to consequences. This shift in angle can alleviate the burden of vain self-blame.

Moreover, the "all-or-now not anything" thinking sample has a bent to polarize conditions into extremes. Overcoming self-doubt calls for embracing nuance and recognizing the solar sunglasses of grey in diverse factors of existence. Understand that setbacks or errors don't define your whole nicely well worth or competencies.

A effective method in breaking horrible perception patterns is training self-compassion. Treat your self with the identical kindness and information you will provide a pal dealing with similar demanding conditions. Recognize that everyone makes errors, and these do not decrease your fee as a person.

Mindfulness techniques, together with meditation and deep breathing sporting events, also can play a pivotal position. These practices help bring cognizance to the existing moment, allowing you to check awful mind with out judgment. By developing this highbrow distance, you can pick out no longer to interact with risky perception patterns.

It's critical to venture awful self-talk actively. Replace self-important mind with effective affirmations. For instance, if you entice yourself thinking, "I cannot do that; I usually fail," counteract it with, "I am succesful, and I examine from each enjoy." Consistency in great affirmations allows rewire the mind over time.

Cognitive-behavioral treatment (CBT) techniques are effective in breaking terrible concept styles. Identify particular thoughts that contribute to self-doubt, examine their validity, and reframe them in a more first rate slight. CBT empowers humans to recognize and regulate dangerous cognitive patterns, fostering lasting alternate.

Surrounding your self with a supportive social community is crucial. Share your struggles with relied on buddies or circle of relatives those who can offer encouragement and attitude. External validation and reassurance can counteract the impact of terrible idea patterns.

Setting practical desires and celebrating small victories is every other method. Break down huge obligations into attainable steps, and extensively diagnosed your achievements alongside the manner. This technique builds a enjoy of success and reinforces a outstanding mind-set.

Engaging in sports activities sports that convey pride and fulfillment can counteract self-doubt. Pursue pursuits, workout, or spend time with cherished ones to boost your mood and shift cognizance a long manner from bad mind. Cultivating a terrific environment contributes significantly to breaking terrible idea styles.

Overcoming self-doubt includes a multifaceted technique that addresses horrible concept patterns at their middle. By schooling mindfulness, self-compassion, effective affirmations, and cognitive restructuring, humans can ruin unfastened from the grip of self-doubt and domesticate a extra resilient attitude. Building a robust aid tool and fostering a terrific surroundings further make contributions to the journey of overcoming self-doubt and embracing self-self assure.

www.ingramcontent.com/pod-product-compliance
Lightning Source LLC
Chambersburg PA
CBHW071443080526
44587CB00014B/1976